Benefits in God

Fred Igbeare

WESTBOW
PRESS®
A DIVISION OF THOMAS NELSON
& ZONDERVAN

Scripture taken from the New King James Version®. Copyright © 1982
by Thomas Nelson. Used by permission. All rights reserved.

Scripture taken from the NEW AMERICAN STANDARD BIBLE®, Copyright © 1960, 1962, 1963,
1968, 1971, 1972, 1973, 1975, 1977, 1995 by The Lockman Foundation. Used by permission.

Scripture quotations from The ESV® Bible (The Holy Bible, English Standard Version®),
copyright © 2001 by Crossway. Used by permission. All rights reserved.

Scripture quotations marked (NLT) are taken from the Holy Bible, New Living Translation,
copyright © 1996, 2004, 2007 by Tyndale House Foundation. Used by permission of
Tyndale House Publishers, Inc., Carol Stream, Illinois 60188. All rights reserved.

King James Version (KJV) by Public Domain.

Quotes from Greg Laurie are used by permission. All rights reserved.

Quotes from Norman Geisler are used by permission. All rights reserved.

Quotes from Jack Graham are used by permission. All rights reserved.

This book is a work of non-fiction. Unless otherwise noted, the author and the publisher
make no explicit guarantees as to the accuracy of the information contained in this book
and in some cases, names of people and places have been altered to protect their privacy.

WestBow Press books may be ordered through booksellers or by contacting:

WestBow Press
A Division of Thomas Nelson & Zondervan
1663 Liberty Drive
Bloomington, IN 47403
www.westbowpress.com
1 (866) 928-1240

Because of the dynamic nature of the Internet, any web addresses or links contained
in this book may have changed since publication and may no longer be valid. The views
expressed in this work are solely those of the author and do not necessarily reflect the
views of the publisher, and the publisher hereby disclaims any responsibility for them.

Any people depicted in stock imagery provided by Thinkstock are models,
and such images are being used for illustrative purposes only.
Certain stock imagery © Thinkstock.

ISBN: 978-1-5127-2103-4 (sc)
ISBN: 978-1-5127-2104-1 (hc)
ISBN: 978-1-5127-2102-7 (e)

Library of Congress Control Number: 2015919476

Print information available on the last page.

WestBow Press rev. date: 5/6/2016

Contents

"Bless the LORD, O my soul,

And forget not all His

Benefits..."

(Psalm 103:2, NKJV)

Love – Salvation – Peace – The Holy Spirit – Power – Joy – Born Again – Forgiveness – Hope – Purpose – Rest – Priority – Reconciliation – Success – Confidence – Knowledge – Spiritual Intelligence – Freedom – Prosperity – Prayer – Praise Power – Healing – Protection – Satisfaction – New World

Introduction: God Loves *You*

Benefits in God aims to inform and remind people (unbelievers and believers) about the benefits of embracing God's *love* and sharing it with others.

For unbelievers especially, this book shows why they should pay particular attention to the *true gospel of God*. It is *the good news of great joy, offering peace* between God and humans as well as peace from the troubles of this world. The gospel shows us how we can be *saved from all of our problems*. That includes personal, political, social, economic or spiritual problems. It's the good news of how we can obtain enduring success and everlasting satisfaction with access to the *kingdom of heaven* forever! Praise God!

In the gospel, we find hope for a new life. That's *eternal life* in *abundance,* with *freedom* from the pain, sorrow, decay, sin and death of this world. But there are fake gospels out there that can blind you to the truth. So beware! Don't be deceived. *Get to know the true gospel of God's kingdom.* Then decide whether to accept or reject it. But choose wisely. Don't make your choice based on wrong information or bad intelligence.

Seek rather *spiritual intelligence* from God about life and its issues. Get truthful and deep insights beyond normal human perceptions. Consider carefully and thoughtfully the information presented in this book. Know that God gives everyone a choice between life and death – this book makes the case that choosing life, eternal life, is the best path to everlasting success and fulfillment.

For believers, *Benefits in God* provides a reminder of the beauty and rewards of having a relationship with God. It endeavors to offer deeper insights into the wonderful benefits of being a citizen of heaven, a child of God and a partaker of the divine nature. This book can especially serve as a resource for sharing the good news of great joy with others. It makes the case that those who *sincerely seek God* will find a bounteous harvest of many benefits. These include love, joy, peace, hope, power, confidence, knowledge, success, freedom, prosperity, protection, healing, satisfaction and ultimately, eternal life.

Believers will get to spend eternity with God (in whose presence is fullness of joy and pleasures forever – see Psalm 16:11). God is a fun being who loves us deeply and wants us to inherit the kingdom of heaven with all its joyous glory and abundance. Desiring the best for us, the Lord God takes no pleasure in the misery and destruction of human lives (see Ezekiel 18:32).

A recurring theme in this book is **love**. Because of love, God sent His Son to die for our sins. *Benefits in God* looks at how God wants us to embrace love as a lifestyle, specifically in terms of how we relate to other humans. That is because it is through love that we can overcome sin, which is at the core of our problems. We are *hurting each other under the influence of sin*, instead of *loving each other in accordance with God's law* (see Leviticus 19:17-18, Matthew 22:36-40 and Romans 3:21-26). *Everyone is guilty of sin* except the Son of God (see Romans 3:23 and 2 Corinthians 5:21).

Sin has so tainted us that we don't accurately reflect God's essence: love. As a result, sin destroys our peace, joy, prosperity, freedom and ultimately life, among other things. It is taking this world on a downward spiral to disaster. *Sin puts us at war with our Maker (and each other)*. It corrupts *God's image* in us and terminates life, preventing us from fully enjoying the splendor of God's vast wonderful creations!

But there is good news. *We can have peace with God and freedom from sin.* Because of God's love demonstrated through His Son, humans can gain victory over sin and death. We can come to *fully realize our potential as those created in God's image*. Through the *Holy Spirit,* God can help us to begin the process of becoming more God-like, *more loving* in *perfection* and *holiness.*

A great advantage of making peace with God is that we become *born again* (read more about it in this book). It is only by being born again that we can enter the kingdom of heaven. After the Son of God returns to usher in a new world, *God's kingdom will be the only realm standing.* This world will be destroyed, along with those who do not follow God's way grounded in love. *Benefits in God* shows how we can be part of the new world that God will create. It is a new world free of sorrow, pain, tears, sin and death but full of love, joy, rest, peace and life everlasting. Enjoy!

Acknowledgements: all Praises to God

All thanks go to God for the favor, privilege and vision for writing this book. I am forever grateful for salvation made possible by the incomparable sacrifice on the cross by the Son of God. I thank God for working through the Holy Spirit to shape my life, helping me to become better. I am profoundly grateful for the much-needed insights to navigate the topics in this book. Overall, I thank You Lord for *I know* that you have blessed me beyond measure!

A million thanks indeed go to all those (friends, family or ministers) who have assisted me in various ways in putting together this book. Much gratitude go to God particularly for Joe Focht, senior pastor at Calvary Chapel Philadelphia. I got a pleasant surprise one day when I approached him about the 'Benefits in God' project, initially for an evangelism website. As it turned out, I learnt then that a speaker at the church's recent women's seminar had spoken on a similar topic! Wow! God is certainly good. Pastor Joe then went on to provide me with a copy of the conference CD, a great resource.

Moreover, he later hosted a free apologetics conference at the church. Among the excellent presentations at the conference was one by author Norman Geisler, a most valuable resource quoted thankfully in this book. In addition to Dr. Geisler, I thank God for Greg Laurie and Jack Graham, both ministers of the gospel, who have also graciously granted permission to quote from their writings.

There are, additionally, two other people that I'm especially grateful to God for. Of great benefit has been the feedback and assistance from my dear sister, Grace Ibemere, who made very specific and useful suggestions. At one point, indeed, she and her family hosted me for about three months. They took care of my needs as I focused on writing and rewriting this book. Also, my dear friend and minister of the gospel, Kevin Miles has been a true friend and valued encourager in times of need. We spent many evenings discussing the topics of this book as initially published on an evangelism website. His friendship, insights and feedback have been most helpful. My deepest gratitude also goes to the following friends and ministers for their much appreciated feedback on the book: Leo Akpan, Marcia Dover, Katherine Joyce-Reilly, Luke Mason, Cecilia N'jie, Bill Ricker, Vivian Shackleford and Tony Tilford.

Over the years, my grasp of the gospel has grown tremendously from listening to, learning from and observing certain ministers (up close or from afar). I thank God for using them to enrich my life. Some have gone on to be with the Lord like my dear Uncle Mercy Igbeare (a most loving minister of the gospel), Kenneth Ware (overseeing pastor of the Brooklyn Tabernacle's Prayer Band ministry when I served there) and Carlo Boerkstaaf (who preached so deeply multiple Friday nights at the Prayer Band meetings – enriching and unforgettable). Also quite memorable were Sister Ware's praise and worship songs, resounding and reverberating many, many years beyond those Friday nights.

Special thanks, furthermore, go to God for Jim Cymbala, senior pastor at the Brooklyn Tabernacle, for his selfless service and sincere devotion to preaching the gospel. With a heart for prayer and reliance on the power of the Holy Spirit, Pastor Cymbala's desire is to see people get saved no matter their status or race. (For what it means to be "saved" please see the chapter titled "Salvation: Life in Abundance Forever".) What a great example of ministry to observe firsthand!

Others I am grateful to God for include: Enoch A. Adeboye, Sonny Arguinzoni, Emmanuel A. Bada, A.R. Barnard, Nicky Cruz, Carol Cymbala (Brooklyn Tabernacle Choir), Michael Durso, Tony Evans, Dotun Gboyega, David Geisler, Billy Graham, Charles Hammond, Myrna Hammond, Jack Hayford, Georgina Hill (Royal Family Kids Camp), Mark Hill (RFKC), I.V. Hilliard, David Ireland, David Jeremiah, Brother Joe, Eric Lambert, Jr., John MacArthur, Tyrone McDonald, Donnie McClurkin, Joyce Meyer, Joel Osteen, Brian Pettrey, Mac Powell (Third Day), Lloyd Pulley, Raul Riese, Michael W. Smith, Zollie L. Smith, Jr., R. C. Sproul, Charles Stanley, Lee Strobel, Charles R. Swindoll, Al Toledo, Anthony L. Trufant, Ed Young, Sr., Ravi Zacharias and many, many others. Any omission is an error on my part – please forgive me!

May God bless you all abundantly!

– Fred Igbeare

Chapter 1

Love

Love: Children of God and Partakers of the Divine Nature

Highlights:

- God loves us despite our faults, frailties and failures, offering to help us overcome our limitations so we can gain everlasting life, success, satisfaction and other great benefits in God.
- *We don't need to be perfect or holy to come to God.* A loving God gives us a fresh start when we become saved (believers), using the Holy Spirit to enhance us with the love, power and self-control needed for the new and abundant life forever – praise God!
- God's love opens the door for believers to enter a coming new world of joy, peace, rest and righteousness in the kingdom of heaven. Believers get to be:
    - (1) unique royalty as children of God,
    - (2) partakers of the divine nature in love, perfection and holiness,
    - (3) conduit of God's love to others,
    - (4) citizens in the kingdom of heaven,
    - (5) heirs of God and joint heirs with Jesus Christ, the true King of kings,
    - (6) recipients of a new spiritual, incorruptible body, and
    - (7) beneficiaries of a coming new and better world to live in God's perfect presence forever – praise the Lord!

1

When a tornado hit his home, wreaking havoc, Don Lansaw moved fast. Using his body as shield, he swiftly covered his wife Bethany. That move saved her life – but he did not survive. To protect her out of love, he had sacrificed himself for his wife. Afterward, the grateful wife described her brave husband as her hero (Roth, 2011).

To surrender one's life to save another is undoubtedly the greatest act of love (see John 15:13). What Don did for his wife that day reminds me of a fascinating day in human history. On a Roman cross many years ago, Jesus Christ gave up His life to save us all. *He is my ultimate hero:* not Superman, not Batman, not Spider-Man or even Iron Man. These are all fictional heroes, but *Jesus is real!* And they don't even come close to the supernatural powers Jesus Christ controls to rescue and save human beings (see John 10:17-18).

The Kingdom of Heaven

The Son of God died to save you and me from our sins, which are at the core of humanity's problems. Jesus died to give us the joy, peace and beauty of eternal life with God in the kingdom of heaven. He died to save us from the pains, sorrows and death of this world. Those who are saved get to partake in the kingdom of God, the only realm that will supersede this world, which is destined for destruction.

Only God's perfect kingdom will remain standing in the coming new age. It will replace all corrupted governments, societies or entities in this world. God's kingdom brings righteousness, peace and joy everlasting for those who can get in. *Those who get in avoid the second death* and the coming end of this world. Believers are saved ultimately from the wrath of God against sin.

Jesus, who is Himself without sin, is our atonement for sin. He paid on our behalf the penalty for sin, which is death. By rising from the dead afterward, He opened the door for believers to be resurrected to live with God forever when He returns. We get to enjoy the full benefits of the incorruptible, joyful and everlasting life with God. Death has forever lost its power over humans who believe in God! And that is, only by God's grace!

Why Me?

Because of God's love demonstrated through Jesus Christ, you can be equipped to cope with the travails of this world. Moreover, you can escape the impending destruction of this world. You can be part of the coming new world. It's a new world order under God's direct rule free of sin, death, pain and sorrows but full of love, joy, peace, beauty, pleasures and wonders!

"Why me?" you may wonder. "Why did the Son of God die for me?" The answer is simple: **God loves you**. You are created in His image: *male and female* alike (Genesis 1:26-27). You are invaluable, worth more to God than you may imagine. God values you so much that even "the very hairs of your head are all numbered" (Matthew 10:30, New King James Version: NKJV).

God's love is inexorable. It is powerful. No sacrifice is too big for God's love! As an early follower of Jesus Christ, the apostle Paul, wrote in Romans 8:32 (NKJV): "He who did not spare His own Son, but delivered Him up for us all, how shall He not with Him also freely give us all things?"

This is the extent of God's love for us: He is willing to *give us all things* (see also Revelation 21:7). We get to inherit the vast expanse of God's wonderful, endless creations. To enable us obtain our divine inheritance, God has gone to great lengths to redeem us from the devastations and sorrows that sin and death have wrought upon the human race.

New World: Everlasting Love and Peace

Because *God is love* (1 John 4:8), it is His nature to love you. He takes no pleasure and gains nothing from the destruction of human lives through sin (see Ezekiel 18:32). God desires for us all to be saved from sin and death. That is why Jesus Christ took the hit for us all. *His sacrifice makes it possible for us to get access to God through the Holy Spirit* (see Ephesians 2:18). And with access to God, we have access to all that we need to overcome human problems.

Indeed, with Jesus Christ we have peace with God (Romans 5:1). And peace with God grants us access to great and everlasting benefits in God. Those who are saved (believers in God) get to inherit a new and better world free from sin and death – praise God! Believers get to live forever in endless love and peace (see the chapters of this book titled: "Peace beyond Understanding" and "New World: No More Sorrow").

Because He loves us, God could not stand aside and allow us to keep suffering and dying from sin without hope in a diseased world. God intends to replace this world with a new and better one (including a new earth) when Jesus Christ returns. At that time, all who are dead will be resurrected. Gladly, those who are saved (that is, believers: *people whose names are written in the Book of Life)* will live forever in the kingdom of heaven.

Sadly, those who are not saved are doomed. By rebelling against God's commandments founded on love, they are rejecting His kingdom and His righteousness. Their sins are not covered by the blood of Jesus Christ (see the chapter: "Forgiveness: Guilty No More, Showing Others Mercy").

A Better Life through Love

Fundamentally, sin counteracts the essence of God's commandments based on love. "For the commandments, 'You shall not commit adultery,' 'You shall not murder,' 'You shall not steal,' 'You shall not bear false witness,' 'You shall not covet,' and if *there is* any other commandment, are *all* summed up in this saying, namely, 'You shall love your neighbor as yourself.' Love does no harm to a neighbor; therefore love *is* the fulfillment of the law" (Romans 13:9-10, NKJV; see also Matthew 22:34-40, Galatians 5:14-15 and Leviticus 19:17-18).

As the verses from the Holy Bible cited above indicate, God's commandments are founded on love. God wants us to walk in love, because without love sin prevails with all of its ugliness and destructiveness. Sin leads to hopelessness as humans work against each other, hurting each other. Propelled by human weaknesses (among them pride, greed and hatred), *sin degrades life.* It shortchanges our dreams, desires and destiny. It limits how far we can go. It traps people in futilities, dooming to failure our attempts to solve human problems without God. Caution: *if we don't address the question of sin and death, all our efforts to solve human problems will be futile.* That is the sad truth.

In opposition to God's way of loving, giving and humility, sin is fueled by human weaknesses that include malice, selfishness and arrogance. It compels humans to hurt each other in conflicts, contentions and wars. Strife becomes the norm as people struggle and suffer outside the protective boundaries of God's commandments based on love. Sin produces an inexorable downward spiral in human history that will see the destruction of this world.

Sin is dangerous. With devastating consequences, it is the attempt by humans to live outside of God's way, God's law grounded in love. When we follow God's way, we can have victory over sin. When we sin, unfortunately, we are in rebellion against God's way. By sinning, we essentially are rejecting the divine directive to love one another and *to do each other no harm* (see Romans 13:9-10).

Regrettably, we all disobey God (Romans 3:23). We all therefore are exposed to human sorrows, troubles, decay and ultimately death. "For the wages of sin is death, but the free gift of God is eternal life in Christ Jesus our Lord" (Romans 6:23, English Standard Version: ESV). Sin carries a huge cost: the loss of eternal life with God, with denial of access to the kingdom of heaven. But thanks be to God for eternal life through Jesus Christ who redeems us from sin and death – praise the Lord!

The Power of God's Love in Victory over Sin and Death

Fortunately, we can have true freedom: redemption from the law of sin and death (see the chapter: "Freedom: Walking in the Way, the Truth and the Life"). The sacrifice by Jesus Christ at the cross gives believers in God tremendous power today over sin through the Holy Spirit. *Sin boils down largely to a lack of power, love and self-control* (discipline or a sound mind). But God helps us to fix these weaknesses through the Holy Spirit, thanks to the atonement for sin by Jesus Christ, providing peace with God.

Supernaturally, God puts the Holy Spirit into those who are saved (see the chapters titled: "The Holy Spirit: Power, Love and Self-Control" and "Salvation: Life in Abundance Forever"). Endowed with the Spirit of power, love and self-control, believers get divine help to change for the better. We get to defeat sin through God's very personal intervention in our hearts.

Assuredly, God's wisdom, mercy and grace are unmatched – praise the Lord! Working perfectly through the Holy Spirit, God pinpoints the ultimate solution that hits precisely at the heart of our human problems (see Jeremiah 17:9-10 and Romans 5:5). The book of Jeremiah helpfully records a shocking truth about the human heart. It's an alarming reality all humans should grasp urgently to help us appreciate how badly we need God's help.

Jeremiah 17:9 states clearly: "The **heart is deceitful** above all things, and **desperately wicked**: who can know it?" (King James Version: KJV, emphasis

5

added). God knows it. And He loves us so much He doesn't leave us to deal with it alone – praise the Lord!

We get supreme help, thankfully, from God to deal with our desperately wicked hearts and fight the battles of this diseased, sinful world. God puts His very own Spirit in those saved to help us love, and hence rise above sin and death. Indeed: "*…God's love has been poured into our hearts through the Holy Spirit who has been given to us*" (Romans 5:5, ESV, emphasis added).

We therefore can thrive and excel to heights of achievements otherwise impossible for mere mortals – praise God! We get to defeat sin through love, by God's grace. Thank You Lord! You are so wise, wonderful, loving and gracious!

The Holy Spirit and Being Born Again

When saved, we become more than ordinary mortals. We become born again by the power of the Holy Spirit. The same Spirit that raised Jesus Christ from the dead comes to dwell within believers. The Spirit gives us a supernatural rebirth, enabling a new life that leads ultimately to complete, permanent, everlasting freedom from sin and death. Significantly, *we must be born again to enter the kingdom of God* (John 3:3-6 – see also the chapter: "Born Again: Rebirth into Eternity, a Fresh Start").

Overall, God's ultimate purpose is that we become free from sin/*death* and full of love/*life* as citizens of heaven. Like a Divine Potter, God seeks to mold us into the image of His Son Jesus. That is the measure of His love for us: to replicate Himself in us! Remember: God *is* love – *like Father, like children.*

Divine Nature: Perfect and Holy in Love

We, like God, can become full of love, perfect and holy. God wants us to become perfect (Matthew 5:43-48) and holy like Himself (Hebrews 12:9-10). The Lord wants us to become exalted like His Son Jesus Christ: "For those whom He foreknew, He also predestined *to become* conformed to the image of His Son, so that He would be the firstborn among many brethren" (Romans 8:29, New American Standard Bible: NASB).

God wants us to share in His divine nature, with access to all the powers and privileges that come with such an exalted position. As an early follower of Jesus Christ (the apostle Peter) wrote: "Grace and peace be multiplied to you in the knowledge of God and of Jesus our Lord, as *His divine power has given to us all things that pertain to life and godliness*, through the knowledge of Him who called us by glory and virtue by which have been given to us exceedingly great and precious promises, that through these *you may be partakers of the divine nature*, having escaped the corruption that is in the world through lust" (2 Peter 1:2-4, NKJV, emphasis added).

Significantly, those saved become children of God (see John 1:12). "And if children, then heirs; heirs of God, and joint-heirs with Christ; if so be that we suffer with him, that we may be also glorified together," wrote the apostle Paul (Romans 8:17, KJV). Additionally: "Behold what manner of love the Father has bestowed on us, that we should be called children of God," wrote the apostle John, another early disciple of Jesus (1 John 3:1, NKJV; see also Ephesians 2:19-22 and Ephesians 5:1-2).

God cares for us so much that He wants us to be part of His divine royal family. God's children are divine royalty, unlike anything the world has ever seen: "But you are not like that, for you are a chosen people. You are *royal priests, a holy nation*, God's very own possession. As a result, *you can show others the goodness of God*, for he called you out of the darkness into his wonderful light." (1 Peter 2:9, New Living Translation: NLT, emphasis added; see also Psalm 82:6).

All are Invited into God's Family

Everyone is invited to join God's family. "For God so loved the world that He gave His only begotten Son, that *whoever believes in Him* should not perish but have everlasting life" (John 3:16, NKJV, emphasis added). Moreover: "But as many as received Him, to them He gave the right to become children of God, to those who believe in His name: who were born, not of blood, nor of the will of the flesh, nor of the will of man, but of God" (John 1:12-13, NKJV).

The invitation is for everyone to come to God to be born again and filled with the Holy Spirit, the Spirit of power, love, disciple (self-control), knowledge and truth. Note that we don't need to be perfect to come to God (there would be no need for us to become perfect, *if we were already perfect)!* God loves us even in our sinful state (Romans 5:8), desiring however that we change for the better through love onto perfection and holiness (see Matthew 5:43-48 and Hebrews 12:10). Indeed, Jesus Christ died for sinners not the righteous (see Matthew 9:13 and Mark 2:17).

Assuredly, He died for all sinners all throughout time. That includes those who lived and died before Jesus took on human bodily form. John 1 describes how Jesus was the Word that was with God in the beginning and *was God*. This indicates that all interactions of humanity with God throughout time involved the Son of God. Out of love, God designed the plan of salvation before the foundation of this world which covers everyone (see 1 Peter 1:17-21, Romans 2:12-16, Revelation 13:7-10, John 3:16, Jeremiah 17:9-10 and Revelation 2:23).

No one is left out. Those covered by the salvation plan include the multitudes that died before the crucifixion and resurrection of Jesus Christ. They include Abraham (see Galatians 3:8), Moses, David, Daniel, Joseph and others who did not reject God's law, His way.

Importantly, even on a basic level, through the conscience, God has provided a means for people to tell right from wrong. See Romans 2 for more information (especially Romans 2:15-16). So there is no excuse for harming your neighbor in contravention of God's law based on love.

God's Personal Touch: Helping Us to Love

Thankfully, in the plan of salvation, God is willing to invest in us personally. He goes beyond just showing us the right way. That's the way of love, perfection and holiness through the teachings in the Holy Bible. God helps us *to do* His will, to follow His way based on love.

Under the direction of the Holy Spirit, the Lord helps believers to rise above our human limitations. God knows we are weak and need the help of the Holy Spirit. The Lord understands how much better we would be if *we all* learned to love each other more. Certainly, the world would be a much better place if people loved more. Not just more, but *love perfectly*.

The Beauty of Experiencing and Sharing God's Love

A great beauty of experiencing God's love is that He bestows on those saved an overflow of that love. We are to share God's love, by showing "others the goodness of God" (1 Peter 2:9, NLT) as we are enabled by the Holy Spirit. By sharing love, which *is* at the core of God's commandments, we can help reduce the spread of sin. *While sin contravenes God's commandments, love counteracts sin.*

"Hatred stirs up strife, But love covers all sins" (Proverbs 10:12, NKJV; see also 1 Peter 4:7-10 and Leviticus 19:17-18)

Fundamentally, you get saved by virtue of God's love, and have the responsibility to share that love (not hatred) with others. In fact, to obey God's law and avoid falling into sin, there are basically two commandments to follow. *Firstly, love God with all your heart, all your soul and all your mind* (Matthew 22:37). *Secondly, love others like yourself* (Matthew 22:39): "On these two commandments hang all the Law and the Prophets," Jesus noted (as quoted in Matthew 22:40, NKJV; see also Deuteronomy 6:5 and Leviticus 19:17-18).

Interestingly, both commandments are inseparable. To do the first (love God) is to do the second (love people) – see 1 John 4:19-21. Basically, the commandments of God boil down to (i) **loving God**, (ii) **loving people**, and (iii) **obeying God**, in a self-reinforcing circle.

- For to love God is to love people (1 John 4:19-21), and
- To love God is to obey God (John 14:23 and 1 John 2:4-5; see also John 3:36).

Notably, our love for God is proven by how well we love others. "If someone says, 'I love God,' and hates his brother, he is a liar; for he who does not love his brother whom he has seen, how can he love God whom he has not seen? And this commandment we have from Him: that he who loves God *must* love his brother also," wrote the apostle John (1 John 4:20-21, NKJV).

Love and Freedom

Love frees us. By following God's law to love people, we can overcome the generational entrapment of sin that leads to so much worldly sorrows. By aligning ourselves with God's law based on love, we come under the law of the Spirit of life in Jesus Christ. We therefore are freed from the law of sin and death (see Romans 8:1-2 and the chapter of this book: "Freedom: Walking in the Way, the Truth and the Life").

We consequently can come to freely flourish forever in love, joy and peace, able to fully enjoy all of our benefits in God. We can come ultimately to reflect truly the image of God in love, perfection and holiness for eternity – praise God!

By God's grace, when Jesus Christ returns, believers get to inherit the kingdom of heaven (see Matthew 25:31-34). God's kingdom frees us from all of our faults, frailties and failures on this earth, this world. We are to get a new earth. Believers also get to ***inherit a perfect new body***, free of corruption, decay and death – praise God!

God knows the frailties of our earthly bodies, battered by the curse and consequences of sin. Because He loves us, he intends eventually to free us from our present bodily limitations. We will be like the Son of God when He returns: perfect and holy – "fashioned like unto his glorious body" (Philippians 3:21, KJV; see also 1 John 3:2).

God's Love Forever

God loves us so much that He gave His Son to die for our sins while we were still sinners! How much more then is that love revealed to us in greater measures when we truly become children of God! Expect more! Expect a whole new world of benefits unending when you embrace God's love and commit to spreading that love to other humans.

Expect blessings everlasting. Expect to be part of the winning team that will inherit the kingdom of heaven. Expect your *great reward from God who has limitless riches to offer* those who walk in His way, in His love. Expect to *live in the loving presence of God*, full of joy and pleasures forever. Expect to enjoy the wonders of God's endless love – praise the Lord!

Finally, my prayer is for the Lord to "direct your hearts into the love of God, and into the patient waiting for Christ" (2 Thessalonians 3:5, KJV). Amen!

Reference

- Roth, Z. (2011). Husband gave life to save wife from tornado — 'He was my hero'. *Yahoo News The Lookout*. Retrieved from http://news.yahoo.com/blogs/lookout/husband-gave-life-save-wife-tornado-hero-153929405.html; ylt=AwrBT.TCxAhV1 8ARF3BGOd ; ylu=X3oDMTE0b2gwZGxjBHNlYwNzcgRwb3 MDMQRjb2xvA2JmMQR2dGlkA1RBVVMwOTdfMQ--

Discussion Questions

1. What is true love and how does God through Jesus Christ show it? Why does God require *you* to show your love for Him by loving others? And how can you love others according to the Word of God?

2. What does it mean to be a child of God, a joint heir with Jesus Christ and a citizen of heaven?

3. Why does God want you to become perfect and holy, a partaker of the divine nature? How can the Holy Spirit help you in this regard?

Chapter 2

Salvation

Salvation: Life in Abundance Forever

Highlights:

- Salvation means your name is written in the Book of Life. By God's grace, believers overcome sin and death, inheriting the kingdom of heaven with all its great benefits forever – praise God!
- There will be a final judgment by Jesus Christ on behalf of God: we all are accountable for whatever we have done on earth.
- Those saved (believers in God) receive the abundant life to enjoy eventually in God's presence a fullness of joy and pleasures forever with no more sorrows, pain or death – not so for the unsaved (nonbelievers).

Nicky Cruz was a gangster. And no ordinary one. He was leader of the Mau Maus, a dreaded street gang in Brooklyn, New York, where violence and death shadowed his troubled steps. At one point, a close friend and fellow gang member got killed, a vicious casualty of a deadly lifestyle. It seemed only a matter of time before Nicky himself would end up likewise.

His doom was certain. That is until he met a loving and persistent preacher in David Wilkerson. He even threatened to kill the preacher! Fortunately, at a rally held by Wilkerson later, Nicky embraced the gospel of salvation. Praise God!

Transformed Mindset: from Hate to Love

Nicky went on to become an evangelist. Changed deeply by the gospel of peace, he has been bringing hope and comfort to many all over the world, sharing the love of God. Retold on screen and in print (*The Cross and the Switchblade*), his story demonstrates the power of God's love expressed through others. God's love can transform lives for the better forever.

God is able to redeem people doomed to condemnation, granting them salvation for eternal life. Nicky's redemption was particularly poignant, considering that his parents were deeply involved in sorcery. Moreover, even his own mother referred to him as belonging to Satan (read more in his book *Run Baby Run*).

Angry, bitter and hateful, Nicky had been committed to hurting people. But God changed all that. Significantly, with salvation comes a transformation of people's perspective and preoccupation in this world. As happened to Nicky, *salvation can transform your mindset from hurting people to loving them, helping them.* It lines you up with God's way of love, opening the door for you into the kingdom of heaven.

The Book of Life

Ultimately, *salvation ensures that by God's grace your name is written in the Book of Life.* You therefore avoid the second death. As a believer in God, you have a place in the new world when God judges this world finally through Jesus Christ (see John 5:24-27, as well as John 14:2-3). At that time, "Death and Hades" would be "cast into the lake of fire. This is *the second death*. And anyone not found written in the Book of Life was cast into the lake of fire," so wrote the apostle John, in visions of future events recorded in the Holy Bible (Revelation 20:14-15, NKJV, emphasis added).

A Coming Day of Judgment:
Eternal Life or the *Second Death?*

A time of judgment is coming. It's inevitable! "And as it is appointed unto men once to die, but after this the judgment" (Hebrews 9:27, KJV). When you become saved, you avoid being condemned at the judgment to the second death, the ultimate penalty for sin. "For *the wages of sin is death*, but the *free gift of God is eternal life in Christ Jesus* our Lord" (Romans 6:23, NASB, emphasis added).

When Jesus Christ returns, all the dead will be resurrected. "Do not marvel at this; for an hour is coming, in which all who are in the tombs will hear His voice, and will come forth; those who did the good *deeds* to a **resurrection of life**, those who committed the evil *deeds* to a **resurrection of judgment**" (John 5:28-29, NASB, bold emphasis added).

Those saved get to inherit the limitless benefits of God's kingdom. Believers gain eternal life, enjoying the presence of God in fullness of joy and pleasures forever. But those who are **not** saved will perish forever. "These shall be **punished with everlasting destruction** from the presence of the Lord and from the glory of His power" (2 Thessalonians 1:9, NKJV, bold emphasis added: see also Matthew 25:31-46).

Who Pays for Your Debt?

The ultimate penalty for sin is *"everlasting destruction"*. Unfortunately, we've all sinned (Romans 3:23). We all therefore *owe a debt for sin* because we choose to go our own way instead of God's way grounded in love. There are two paths to paying off the debt from sin (see Romans 6:23, NASB):

(1) Pay it yourself with your life (you forfeit everything: "the wages of sin is death").

(2) Or let Jesus Christ pay it for you (you get everything because of His sacrifice: "the free gift of God is eternal life").

My recommendation is option two. By it, the righteousness of Jesus Christ gets credited to your account, covering your sin-debt (see Philippians 3:9 and Romans 3:21-25). In option two, you find salvation: freedom from the second death, a fate so terrible that God saw it fit to send His Son to die in our place.

There is a clear choice: (a) Jesus pays the debt – *get eternal life*; or (b) you pay it yourself – *get "everlasting destruction"* (see 2 Thessalonians 1:9, NKJV). The choice is between life (in abundance) and death (in perdition). So choose wisely.

Choose Eternal Life!

God prefers that we choose eternal life. "For I have no pleasure in the death of anyone, declares the Lord God; so turn, and live" (Ezekiel 18:32, ESV). The Lord does *not* want anyone to end up in the lake of fire. Jesus died so we don't have to. Perfect and sinless, the Son of God took on our punishment at the cross. He thus paid in full the penalty for sin. In a merciful act, He has served our sentence of death. Salvation therefore is easy and free to all.

In a miraculous exchange, those who become saved *get the sinless nature of Jesus Christ credited to their account*. In essence, the saved get the righteousness of Jesus Christ. Believers are blessed with freedom from eternal condemnation – praise God! With that freedom comes access to the kingdom of heaven for a joy-filled life everlasting.

How to Become Saved Now

Why miss out on the eternal benefits in God? It is best for you to become saved (*if you are not already*). All that's needed now is that "you confess with your mouth the Lord Jesus and believe in your heart that God has raised Him from the dead, you will be saved" (Romans 10:9, NKJV). *It is as simple as 1-2-3!*

Just be sincere about the confession for God can tell what's in your heart. "I, the Lord, search the heart, I test the mind, Even to give every man according to his ways, According to the fruit of his doings" (Jeremiah 17:10, NKJV). So there's no point trying to fake it. Most certainly, you must have *sincere faith.*

In addition, *it doesn't matter how bad or evil you may have been.* No matter what, Jesus Christ died for you too. "For whosoever shall call upon the name of the Lord shall be saved" (Romans 10:13, KJV; see also Joel 2:32, Romans 2:12-16, 1 Peter 1:18-21 and John 1). Note: the word "whosoever" includes *everyone.* So there should be no excuse.

Our Conscience and Those Who Died
Before the Resurrection

Everyone *is covered* by God's salvation plan. That includes those who lived and died before Jesus Christ took on humanly form, before His death and resurrection. God has made provisions for all peoples. For instance, as the

15

apostle Paul wrote: "…in that they show the work of the Law written in their hearts, *their conscience bearing witness* *and their thoughts alternately accusing or else defending them,* **on the day when,** according to my gospel, **God will judge** the secrets of men *through Christ Jesus…*" (Romans 2:15-16, NASB, emphasis added, bold and italic).

There's definitely no excuse for doing harm to other humans because *God has given each of us a conscience.* We can tell the difference between right and wrong, love and hatred or good and evil. We are created certainly for *good works,* **not** evil works (see Ephesians 2:10). When we ignore our conscience to persist in evil works, we set ourselves up for eternal failure. When we ignore loving our neighbors as ourselves, we open ourselves up to eternal condemnation.

So beware. There's really no excuse. And as the apostle Paul wrote: "The aim of our charge is *love* that issues from a *pure heart* and a *good conscience* and a *sincere faith*" (1 Timothy 1:5, ESV, bold emphasis added; see also 2 Corinthians 1:12, Acts 24:16 and Acts 23:1). God's wisdom is definitely beyond measure. It is quite amazing the brilliance of giving each human a conscience: "their conscience bearing witness" (see Romans 2:15-16, NASB; see also Deuteronomy 30:11-14).

From my perspective, for the conscience to 'bear witness' there is some sort of recording (logging) of our innate, internal decision-making process. Some sort of videotaping technology or 'conscience logs' too advanced for humans to grasp? Perhaps! Anyway, God knows how it's being done (see Jeremiah 17:9-10). So on judgement day, no one can claim God is unfair or unjust. A playback of what has been recorded or logged would be quite revealing. Even our secret thoughts or actions cannot be hidden from God (see 1 Corinthians 4:5, Luke 12:2 and Luke 8:17).

Overall, God is too loving to let people perish without giving them opportunities to be saved. Even the wise men (magi) from the east found a way through divine revelation to come to see and worship the baby Jesus (Matthew 2). So beware and don't be deceived by false arguments that disregard God's interaction with peoples of all nations throughout the ages (see Romans 1:19-32).

Come *as You are* to God

And please ***don't wait till you become perfect to come to God.*** Perfection is not required. In fact, *Jesus died for imperfect people:* "…For I did not come to call the righteous, but sinners, to repentance" (Matthew 9:13, NKJV). Just come as you are. *Don't wait to be cleaned up. God will do the cleaning,* and begin the process of making things right in your life.

Certainly, when you become saved, the benefits are marvelous and eternal. You come to have the eternity perspective. God enables you to discern that this world is passing away. You therefore come to understand that your problems in it won't last anyway, if you are saved. You have hope and confidence in God for eternity.

The Lord gives you *a limitless capacity to cope and thrive* despite the problems of this world. You become empowered to succeed forever. No obstacles or troubles can stop you – praise God! Indeed, God guarantees your inheritance in the new world where perfection and satisfaction for believers are fully realized. You get to inherit the glorious kingdom of heaven. Think on that.

The Abundant Life and God's Way of Love

In Jesus Christ, you get access to heavenly resources available only to those saved. You come to be in a place of divine security and serenity where nothing can rob you of the abundant life as God desires it. And as Jesus noted, "The thief does not come except to steal, and to kill, and to destroy. *I have come that they may have life*, and that *they may have it more abundantly*" (John 10:10, NKJV, emphasis added).

God did not intend for us to suffer. He wants us to live in abundance, not in want and dismay. We are supposed to have dominion over God's creation on earth (Genesis 1:26). But humans have instead become slaves to sin and death. What a great tragedy!

We are supposed to have the fullness of life and joy. But we are forced to continually struggle for survival despite all these centuries of human endeavors to advance. Human sorrow, decay and death have become our story. Many people lack even the basics of life. This is in a world awash with plenty. Why?

It is *because God's way of love is greatly absent from our lives.* Malice, arrogance and selfishness abound instead. We all are reaping the consequences of such wrong choices, such misdirected human endeavors in a debased, diseased and damaged world. But there is hope. Salvation from God opens the door for us all to experience truly the abundant life as God desires it.

Make Your Peace with God Now

If you haven't already done so, please make your peace with God now. Get divine help to overcome all of your troubles now! Accept God's offer of salvation and get access to the abundant life – make the right move now. *Come to God in repentance* and be saved.

Please say this prayer: "*Dear God, please come into my life and save me from sin and death. I desire the abundant life. Help me please. I admit I am a sinner, and acknowledge that Jesus Christ, my Lord and Savior, died for my sins and was resurrected by the power of the Holy Spirit. Please fill me up with the Holy Spirit so that I can live to do Your will, spreading Your love to others. In Jesus name I pray. Amen!*"

Discussion Questions

1. What does it mean to be saved? How can you get saved? What are the requirements for salvation? What do you have to do (or not do)? How about those who died before Jesus Christ came in human form – how are they covered?

2. Why is salvation so important? Does being saved mean all your troubles will disappear instantly? When will believers experience the full joy of salvation? And why did King David pray to God in Psalm 51:12 (ESV): "Restore to me the joy of your salvation"?

3. What does it mean to have eternal life and escape the second death – what is the alternative? Why does God *not* want us to experience the second death?

Chapter 3

Peace

Peace beyond Understanding

Highlights:

- The peace of God in all conditions bestows calmness, confidence and restfulness upon those saved.
- Peace with God means that the vast sin-filled gap – the gulf between God and humans – is bridged, opening the way for believers to have the joys of enduring fellowship with the Creator.
- Peace with God brings forgiveness of sin, protection from the second death and a place in the eternal kingdom of heaven for believers to enjoy all of its unending benefits.

It did not look good. A windstorm raged, sending waves beating into and filling their boat. Threatening to capsize the boat *and* their faith, the danger was real. They were afraid. Yet, despite the disturbance and their desperation, there was One amongst them who *slept peacefully* on a pillow in the boat. What a contrast! Waking Him though, they asked (Mark 4:38, NKJV): "Teacher, do You not care that we are perishing?"

When He arose, He did something quite amazing. Rebuking the wind, He spoke to the sea: "Peace, be still!" Instantly, the wind stopped. And "there was a great calm" (Mark 4:39, NKJV). Wow!!! He then asked why they were so fearful, lacking in faith. Speaking to one another, they wondered: "Who can this be, that even the wind and the sea obey Him" (Mark 4:41, NKJV)?

The Prince of Peace

The One they spoke of that day is the Prince of Peace foretold by the Prophet Isaiah: "For unto us a child is born, unto us a son is given: and the government shall be upon his shoulder: and his name shall be called Wonderful, Counsellor, The mighty God, The everlasting Father, The Prince of Peace" (Isaiah 9:6, KJV – see also the chapter of this book titled: "Good News of Great Joy").

He is the One who has the power to command the winds and to calm the storms in your life, both external and internal. He *is* our peace through the storms of this world, reconciling us to God and bridging the vast sin-filled gap between the Creator and the created. He is Jesus Christ, the Son of God: "for through Him we both have our *access in one Spirit to the Father*" (Ephesians 2:18, NASB, emphasis added; see also Ephesians 2:14).

Peace with Our Maker

Through Him, we have peace with our Maker for salvation: "Therefore being justified by faith, we have peace with God through our Lord Jesus Christ" (Romans 5:1, KJV). A priceless benefit of having peace with God is that it solves a great problem, a great divide that separates us from the Creator. That separation is bridged at the cross with the atonement for our sin by Jesus Christ. The bridge grants those saved (believers) access to immeasurable benefits in God denied mankind because of sin.

Sin is like a drop of sewage in a cup of purified water – it corrupts. It kills. A pure, perfect and Holy God cannot be expected to *tolerate forever* such corruption which diminishes, degrades and destroys human life. Sadly, sin brings with it a curse, a debt burden payable by death, including this disturbing and dreadful consequence: "'*There is* no peace,' says the Lord, 'for the wicked'" (Isaiah 48:22, NKJV). But through Jesus Christ, God provides salvation. We can have peace, with the debt paid in full – praise God! You don't have to worry about it or carry that burden anymore (see the chapter of this book titled "Rest from Your Burdens").

The sacrifice by Jesus Christ at the cross means that once saved your sins are erased – your slate is wiped clean (see also the chapter of this book titled: "Forgiveness: Guilty No More, Showing Others Mercy"). You have a fresh, new start in life and can withstand the storms of this world, no matter how big or bad. Like Jesus, you can even sleep peacefully through any storm – praise God! And by God's grace, you are assured of a place in the coming new world, blessed with the joys of eternal life.

Internal and External Storms: the Peace of God

Meanwhile, in this passing world that is headed for destruction, the peace of God covers you. It fortifies you to cope with the internal and external turmoil, the damaging conflicts that come from the curse of sin. You get a sense of calmness, of peace that only God can provide.

You are therefore able to embrace this injunction: "Be anxious for nothing, but in everything by prayer and supplication, with thanksgiving, let your requests be made known to God; *and the peace of God, which surpasses all understanding*, will guard your hearts and minds through Christ Jesus" (Philippians 4:6-7, NKJV, emphasis added).

It is a peace that reaches into the deepest fiber of your being, giving you a reassurance that no matter what happens, God has you covered. As a child of God, you have the Holy Spirit inside of you. The Spirit strengthens and guides you, helping you through *all the struggles that we humans must face*. The difference is that as a believer in God, you have one huge edge – an infinite advantage: the power of God helps you.

Nothing to Fear or Worry About

You have nothing to worry about. All that you need to do is *focus on seeking the kingdom of God and His righteousness* (see Matthew 6:33 and the chapter of this book: "Priority Number One: God – His Kingdom and His Righteousness"). And **God will take care of your every need.** You have nothing to fear or fret about. "In peace I will both lie down and sleep, For You alone, O LORD, MAKE ME TO DWELL IN SAFETY" (Psalms 4:8, NASB).

Moreover, as Isaiah 26:2-4 (NKJV) states:

> "Open the gates,
> That the righteous nation which keeps the truth may enter in.
> You will keep *him* in perfect peace,
> *Whose* mind *is* stayed *on You,*
> Because he trusts in You.
> Trust in the LORD forever,
> For in YAH, the LORD, *is* everlasting strength."

Moreover, as Jesus told His early disciples: "Peace I leave with you; my peace I give to you. Not as the world gives do I give to you. Let not your hearts be troubled, neither let them be afraid" (John 14:27, ESV). My wish for you then (quoting 1 Thessalonians 5:23-24, KJV) is that "the very God of peace sanctify you wholly; and I pray God your whole spirit and soul and body be preserved blameless unto the coming of our Lord Jesus Christ"! Amen!

Discussion Questions

---

1. What does it mean to have peace with God? And how is it related to the peace of God?

2. How does God enable you to have and maintain peace through the storms of this world?

3. Why is God's peace available only to those who are saved, that is: those who believe in God (those whose names are written in the Book of Life)? And how is your answer related to Ephesians 2:14-18?

Chapter 4

The Holy Spirit

The Holy Spirit: Power, Love and Self-Control

Highlights:

- The Holy Spirit comes to dwell within each believer, providing the **divine power** needed for victory over all of our troubles as we obey God's commandments centered in love.
- The Spirit empowers believers to **love others deeply** and counteract the disruptive pull of sin in hatred, greed and pride that has produced such devastating strife among humans.
- Through the Holy Spirit, God provides the wherewithal for believers to exercise **self-control or discipline** over the excesses that typically lure humans into trouble.

Something quite wonderful happened one day in Jerusalem. The disciples of Jesus Christ were gathered expectantly "all with one accord" after He had ascended onto heaven. "And suddenly there came a sound from heaven, as of a rushing mighty wind, and it filled the whole house where they were sitting. Then there appeared to them divided tongues, as of fire, and *one* sat upon each of them. And they were all filled with the Holy Spirit…" (Acts 2:1-4, NKJV). Praise God!

Filled with the Holy Spirit, they were now imbued with power from God, emboldened to do good and great works. Indeed, those filled with the Holy Spirit don't have to live in fear, mediocrity or sin anymore. With the Spirit, believers obtain the power, love and discipline needed to walk in God's way. "For God has not given us a spirit of fear, but of power and of love and of a sound mind" (2 Timothy 1:7, NKJV; see also the ESV and NASB translations).

Heightened by fears, unfortunately, our sinful nature can be quite problematic. It disrupts our peaceful coexistence with each other. Sin indeed prevents the realization of our full potentials as those created in God's image. It brings death.

But by God's grace through the Holy Spirit, thankfully, believers can overcome sin's limitations. By the Spirit *through Jesus Christ, we have access to God* and are freed from the law of sin and death (see Ephesians 2:18 and Romans 8:1-2). By God's grace through the Holy Spirit, we become born again, facilitating our rebirth into eternity for the abundant life everlasting (see John 3:3-6 and John 10:10).

Rectifying the absence of Power, Love and Self-Control

Significantly, a supernatural transaction occurs when the Holy Spirit comes upon believers – we become enhanced by God's amazing and limitless power. The Spirit is an enabler, transforming us into victorious over-comers, as believers seek to do God's will and reverse sin's devastation (see Romans 8:7-17 and Galatians 5:16-18). Sin essentially boils down to *the complete absence or limited presence of: (a) power, (b) love and (c) self-control (discipline or a sound mind).* But by the power of the Holy Spirit, we are able to understand and rise above our human weaknesses.

Dwelling in us (1 Corinthians 3:16), the Holy Spirit enables believers to "understand the things freely given us by God" (1 Corinthians 2:12, ESV). Believers are blessed by God with spiritual intelligence, deep insights regarding life, sin and death (see the chapter titled "Spiritual Intelligence: Of Sights and Insights"). Filled with the Holy Spirit, believers become spiritually enhanced, empowered to see and do things that our natural human faculties cannot facilitate or enable – praise God!

A great illustration of this empowerment is retold in David Wilkerson's book *The Cross and the Switchblade* with testimonies from former drug addicts.

They attributed their victory over the deadly habit to their baptism by the Holy Spirit. In fact, one former addict recounted how he tried to go back to the old habit but couldn't. The Holy Spirit restrained him such that the habit had lost its allure – praise God! By God's grace, through the Holy Spirit thankfully, believers are empowered to overcome our limitations, resisting the allure of sin and defeating the forces of evil.

Beyond Water Baptism – the Baptism of the Holy Spirit

Foretelling of a greater event in the life of believers beyond water baptism, John the Baptist spoke: "After me One is coming who is mightier than I, and I am not fit to stoop down and untie the thong of His sandals. I baptized you with water; but *He will baptize you with the Holy Spirit*" (Mark 1:7-8, NASB, emphasis added). John was speaking of the Son of God, Jesus Christ.

Jesus Himself, before ascending to heaven, told His early disciples to expect this transformational experience. "Gathering them together, He commanded them not to leave Jerusalem, but to wait for what the Father had promised, 'Which,' *He said*, 'you heard of from Me; for John baptized with water, but you will be baptized with the Holy Spirit not many days from now" (Acts 1:4-5, NASB).

Spreading the Gospel of God: Sharing Love

Jesus, furthermore, told His early disciples: "But you shall receive power when the Holy Spirit has come upon you; and you shall be witnesses to Me in Jerusalem, and in all Judea and Samaria, and to the end of the earth" (Acts 1:8, NKJV; see also John 16:7-15). Afterwards when the Spirit came upon them in Jerusalem, described above in this chapter's introduction, the disciples became much more emboldened to share the gospel. *Sharing the gospel with others indeed is a key role assigned to all believers.*

Fundamentally, spreading the gospel comes down to *loving others as we share the good news of peace with God.* It is the good news of great joy proclaiming salvation from sin, death and destruction forever. It is a most welcome news of salvation onto eternal life with God. And in God's presence, believers find the fullness of love, joy, peace and pleasures forever. *It is salvation from the wrath of God against sin.* For believers, salvation provides numerous benefits. They include peace, power, success, healing, prosperity, knowledge, satisfaction, spiritual intelligence and, of course, the Holy Spirit, to name a few.

The Divine Helper

Before His departure to heaven, Jesus told His disciples: "But the Helper, the Holy Spirit, whom the Father will send in My name, He will teach you all things, and bring to your remembrance all that I said to you" (John 14:26, NASB). We do indeed need to be taught and reminded about the things of God. There is certainly no shortage of false information or sinful distractions. The Holy Spirit helps keep our focus on God.

In addition, Jesus told the disciples: "But I tell you the truth, it is to your advantage that I go away; for if I do not go away, the Helper will not come to you; but if I go, I will send Him to you. And He, when He comes, will *convict the world concerning sin* and *righteousness* and *judgment…*" (John 16:7-8, NASB, emphasis added).

As the Divine Helper, the Holy Spirit opens up our understanding of scriptures, empowering believers to speak authoritatively to others about faith in God. Fundamentally, that faith is based on obeying the commandments of God centered in love. *Obeying God involves selflessly loving people.* It's a life-changing practice that can improve the lot of all humans if we all did it, without exceptions.

The Fruit of the Spirit

And as you may very well know, some people are easier to love than others. For those you may consider unlovable, or those that may have hurt you deeply, the Holy Spirit can enable you to love them through God's power. *It is a divine empowerment that takes you to a level far above your ordinary capabilities.*

It is instructive to see what comes first in the listing for the fruit of the Spirit (the outcome of being led by the Holy Spirit in our daily existence): "But the fruit of the Spirit is *love, joy, peace, patience, kindness, goodness, faithfulness, gentleness, self-control*; against such things there is no law" (Galatians 5:22-23, NASB, emphasis added). The Spirit bestows upon believers the ability to exhibit these Godly qualities.

Helping us with the self-control (sound mind or discipline) that we need, the Holy Spirit enables believers to avoid falling into sinful habits. Described as "the works of the flesh" by Paul, they are to be avoided. The sinful habits are "adultery, fornication, uncleanness, lewdness, idolatry, sorcery, hatred, contentions, jealousies, outbursts of wrath, selfish ambitions, dissensions, heresies, envy, murders, drunkenness, revelries, and the like; of which I tell you beforehand, just as I also told you in time past, that those who practice such things will not inherit the kingdom of God" (Galatians 5:19-21, NKJV).

May it *not be so with you*. May you indeed inherit the kingdom of God. May you be filled with the Holy Spirit. May you manifest the fruit of the Spirit abundantly. May you lack in no good thing. Overflowing in love, may you be a blessing to multitudes. May you abound in good works. May you inherit all the wonderful treasures in the kingdom of heaven – in Jesus name I pray, amen!

Grounded in Love and the Fullness of God

Furthermore, to quote Paul (Ephesian 3:16-19, NASB), my prayer for you in Jesus name, is that God "would grant you, according to the riches of His glory, to be strengthened with power through His Spirit in the inner man, so that Christ may dwell in your hearts through faith; *and* that you, being rooted and grounded in love, may be able to comprehend with all the saints what is the breadth and length and height and depth, and to know the love of Christ which surpasses knowledge, that you may be filled up to all the fullness of God". Amen!

Discussion Questions

1. How can the Holy Spirit enable you to overcome the challenges and pitfalls in your life? Moreover, from reading 1 Corinthians 15:50 and John 3:1-5, how can the Holy Spirit enable you to enter the kingdom of God? And what is the significance of Ephesians 2:18 (ESV): "For through him we both have access in one Spirit to the Father"?

2. Why is it important for a child of God to love God and other people? How has the absence of more loving people shortchanged the human race? How will things grow worse according to your reading of Matthew 24:12?

3. Why is it critical that people have self-control, discipline or a sound mind? How does the Holy Spirit help us with meeting the laws of God as summarized in: (1) loving God, (2) loving people, and (3) obeying God?

Chapter 5

Power

The Power to Overcome

Highlights:

- Only God has the overwhelming power to overcome all obstacles, solve any problem and defeat any enemy, physical or spiritual.
- By aligning with the one true God, we can become invincible, able to overcome visible and invisible enemies (anything or anyone) including:
    (1) our sin nature,
    (2) other human beings, or
    (3) the spiritual forces of evil.

- And with the most powerful Being in the universe as our Helper, the Heavenly Father (working through His Son, the Holy Spirit and the holy angels), believers can survive and thrive for eternity – praise God!

The situation seemed hopeless. A great army had come up against Jerusalem, its commander spewing taunts and threats. On hearing the bad news, the king of Judah "tore his clothes," put on sackcloth and sought help from God (Isaiah 37:1, NKJV). The invaders had earlier attacked and captured Judah's fortified cities. In a blasphemous letter, moreover, the invading king warned Judah's king not to trust in God for deliverance. That was a colossal mistake!

Desperate Appeal, Swift Response

In appealing to the Lord of heaven and earth, Judah's embattled King Hezekiah said: "Truly, LORD, the kings of Assyria have laid waste all the nations and their lands, and have cast their gods into the fire; for they *were* not gods, but the work of men's hands – wood and stone. Therefore they destroyed them. Now therefore, O LORD our God, save us from his hand, that all the kingdoms of the earth may know that You *are* the LORD, You alone" (Isaiah 37:18-20, NKJV).

God's response was swift and decisive. It demonstrated who has true power to overcome any obstacle or situation, no matter how big or bad. "Then the angel of the LORD went out and struck 185,000 in the camp of the Assyrians; and when men arose early in the morning, behold, all of these were dead. So Sennacherib king of Assyria departed and returned *home* and lived at Nineveh" (Isaiah 37:36-37, NASB).

Sennacherib's story did not end there. "And as he was worshiping in the house of Nisroch his god, Adrammelech and Sharezer, his sons, struck him down with the sword. And after they escaped into the land of Ararat, Esarhaddon his son reigned in his place" (Isaiah 37:38, ESV).

The Greatest Overcoming Power

And Judah, mercifully, was saved from that particular threat. Indeed, *God's power to save* extends far beyond defeating invading armies and humbling arrogant rulers. The Lord's power includes overcoming mankind's last enemy: death! *God's power provides salvation from sin and death.* Salvation is the sure outcome for all who put their faith in God. These are the people who are empowered by the Holy Spirit to obey God's commandments grounded in love.

Under God's power, believers shall never lack in victory. Under God's will, we shall never lack in the power to overcome all obstacles and all enemies. God can do for you what He did for Hezekiah, and much more for eternity. Assuredly, when you become a child of God, you gain access to the greatest overcoming power in the universe. And you can count on that – praise God!

"Besides Me there is no God"

When you become a believer in God, you avoid the eternal doom of those aligned with false gods. You become a part of the royal family of the ***one true God.*** "I *am* the First and I *am* the Last; Besides Me *there is* no God" (Isaiah 44:6, NKJV). Additionally: "...Before Me there was no God formed, And there will be none after Me. I, even I, am the LORD, And there is ***no savior besides Me***" (Isaiah 43:10-11, NASB, bold emphasis added). God *alone* has the power of salvation, to redeem humans from the clutches of sin and death. No other power can.

Moreover, it is only under God's protection, under His superior power that we are shielded from the spiritual forces of evil, seen and *unseen.* "For our struggle is not against flesh and blood, but against the rulers, against the powers, against the world forces of this darkness, against the spiritual *forces* of wickedness in the heavenly *places*" (Ephesians 6:12, NASB). The ultimate way to win against such great forces is, as the apostle Paul noted, to "Put on the full armor of God, so that you will be able to stand firm against the schemes of the devil" (Ephesians 6:11, NASB – see also the chapter: "Protection for Eternal Life").

Power over Our Desperately Wicked Hearts

Significantly, God provides the power to overcome a disease that plagues all humans within: sin (see Romans 7). Note particularly Paul's comments about "sin that dwells in me" (Romans 7:17, NKJV). And as noted in Jeremiah 17:9 (NKJV): "The heart is deceitful above all things, And desperately wicked; Who can know it?" It is only under God's power that we can overcome this dangerous propensity to do wrong that contorts the human heart.

Indeed, "For out of the heart proceed evil thoughts, murders, adulteries, fornications, thefts, false witness, blasphemies" (Matthew 15:19, KJV). But with *the Holy Spirit working within us,* believers can resist this wickedness within and, of course, the external forces of evil that exploit this weakness. Consequently, no adversary can prevail against us – praise God! "You are of God, little children, and have overcome them, because He who is in you is greater than he who is in the world" (1 John 4:4, NKJV)

Divine Help: Power through Prayer

In God, believers find refuge and strength, a most reliable Helper in time(s) of trouble (see Psalm 46:1 and 59:16-17). The Lord God delivers us from dangers not always obvious to normal human perceptions. Without God, we are outgunned, both inwardly and outwardly. The forces of evil are tremendous and unrelenting. To overcome them, *we must seek and accept help* from much greater power(s) found only in God working through Jesus Christ, the Holy Spirit and the holy angels.

To prevail over our numerous challenges and adversaries, prayer is one of our greatest assets (see the chapter "Prayer: Unlimited Access to Heaven"). When he was confronted with an impossible situation above, Hezekiah *prayed to God*. The Lord God acknowledged the king's supplication, telling the besieged ruler through the Prophet Isaiah: "…Because you have prayed to Me about Sennacherib king of Assyria, this is the word that the LORD has spoken against him…" (Isaiah 37:21-22, NASB). Read the rest of the story in the book of Isaiah.

A Very Dangerous Venture

Living without God's help in this terrible world is a very dangerous venture. You and I need to seek God for greater power(s) to survive and flourish. We can, in fact, reach out to God for help anytime. The Lord God is near. **God "is actually not far from each one of us"** (Acts 17:27, ESV, bold emphasis added).

"The LORD is near to all who call upon Him, To all who call upon Him in truth" (Psalms 145:18, NASB). *If we truthfully seek God, we will find Him* and gain salvation from all of our problems in this doomed world. Just call out to Him now, if you are not yet a believer in God! "And it shall come to pass *That* whoever calls on the name of the LORD Shall be saved" (Joel 2:32, NKJV; see also Romans 10:8-13).

For the saved (believers in God), defense against evil is assured: "But the Lord is faithful, who will establish you and guard *you* from the evil one" (2 Thessalonians 3:3, NKJV). Putting His Holy Spirit in you, *if you're a believer*, God will stand with you and for you. The Sovereign Lord has hosts of holy angels to dispatch to help you. He will work with you and love you as you have never been loved before. The Lord will cherish you, nourish you, and build you up step-by-step till you come to realize your full potential as a child of God.

Standing with the Winning Team

Furthermore, God gives you an inheritance that surpasses your imagination, perception and expectations. You get to inherit the kingdom of heaven as a child of the Most High God when Jesus comes back (see Matthew 25:31-34). In the final battle against evil as foretold in the book of Revelation, you stand with the winning team – praise God! The Lord is so powerful He can proclaim the outcome of a war or battle long before it even happens. He is able to bring it to pass, ensuring the defeat of sin, evil, the devil and death: "The last enemy that shall be destroyed is death" (1 Corinthians 15:26, KJV).

To be part of the winning team that inherits the coming new world, we must have faith in God. King Hezekiah trusted in God and was not disappointed. God will not disappoint you. "Trust ye in the LORD for ever: for in the LORD JEHOVAH is everlasting strength" (Isaiah 26:4, KJV). Faith built on believing, trusting and obeying God opens the door for us to be born again, giving us access to everlasting, overcoming power.

"For whatever is born of God overcomes the world; and this is the victory that has overcome the world – our faith" (1 John 5:4, NASB – see also the chapter titled "Born Again: Rebirth into Eternity, a Fresh Start"). Moreover, as noted in the next verse (1 John 5:5, ESV): "Who is it that overcomes the world except the one who believes that Jesus is the Son of God?"

All Authority in Heaven and on Earth: "I Have Overcome the World"

Troubles may come in this world as they did to King Hezekiah, but troubles come to all in mankind anyway. The difference is that the children of God (believers) have an edge: our victory is assured eventually through Jesus Christ. For God has given His Son all authority in heaven and on earth (Matthew 28:18). You have nothing to worry about if you are a child of God, a joint heir with Jesus Christ. Your name is written in the Book of Life. You are saved – praise God!

As Jesus told His early followers: "These things I have spoken to you, that in Me you may have peace. In the world you will have tribulation; but be of good cheer, I have overcome the world" (John 16:33, NKJV). Consider it done. Your victory is guaranteed. So seek God today. Come as you are! If you are not yet saved, know that *you do not need to be perfect or holy to come to God.* God's power will enable you to attain those qualities.

Please call out to God now. Let Him help you overcome the challenges in your life. The Lord can defeat the enemies arrayed against you and equip you with the wisdom, the power to thrive forever. "He stores up sound wisdom for the upright; *He is* a shield to those who walk in integrity, Guarding the paths of justice, And He preserves the way of His godly ones" (Proverbs 2:7-8, NASB).

Let God nourish you with His love, and sustain you by His mightiest of powers to overcome your troubles. God can give you victory over sin and death forever. Call on Him now for eternal life. Cry out to Him for salvation, for protection from the eventual destruction of this world. Don't wait or delay for tomorrow may be too late, for this life is so fickle and can flicker out in an instance.

Besides, it is easy to get saved (see Romans 10:9). So say this prayer now: *Dear God, please come into my life. I acknowledge that I am a sinner – please forgive me my sins. I accept Jesus Christ as my Lord and Savior, and I'm grateful that He has paid the penalty for sin. Please help me. Fill me up with the Holy Spirit so that I can be empowered to do Your will and walk righteously from now on, seeking first Your Kingdom – in Jesus name I pray, amen!*

Discussion Questions

1. What is the problem identified in Romans 7 (especially verses 14-25)? Why does the Bible refer to the human heart as being "desperately wicked" (Jeremiah 17:9) — how does that translate into human conduct you see on a daily basis? And why do all human societies have laws — how do those laws compare to Matthew 22:37-40?

2. Why do you need God's power in you and on your side? What do you need to overcome? What are your impressions from a reading of Romans 6 to 8, and 2 Timothy 1:7? And how can the Holy Spirit help you overcome sin and death?

3. Who are the holy angels? Who are the fallen angels? What are their relationships to each other? How are they involved in human affairs? And why can't we defeat the spiritual forces of wickedness on our own?

Chapter 6

Joy

Good News of Great Joy

Highlights:

- The best news ever for the human race is that salvation from sin and death is available to everyone – believers in God have their names recorded in heaven, written in the Book of Life.
- Joy comes from the benefits of God's presence in our lives *as we obey His commandments grounded in love.*
- Joy is derived furthermore from the knowledge that believers have eternal life in the kingdom of heaven, ultimately free of pain, tears and death, but full of love, joy, peace and other benefits in God.

That wonderful night, the shepherds were out in the fields watching over their flock. They were unaware of what was about to happen. Then "an angel of the Lord suddenly stood before them, and the glory of the Lord shone around them; and they were terribly frightened. But the angel said to them, 'Do not be afraid; for behold, I bring you good news of great joy which will be for all the people'" (Luke 2:9-10, NASB).

The angel continued: "for today in the city of David there has been born for you a Savior, who is Christ the Lord. This *will be* a sign for you: you will find a baby wrapped in cloths and lying in a manger" (Luke 2:11-12, NASB). "And suddenly there was with the angel a multitude of the heavenly host praising God and saying: 'Glory to God in the highest, And on earth peace, goodwill toward men'" (Luke 2:13-14, NKJV)!

The Greatest News of Joy

The announcement that night has been the greatest news of joy ever told to humans. Our Savior had now come – praise God! Jesus came to save us from the hopelessness of this world filled with so much bad news. Everlasting peace would now be in our future by virtue of the birth, subsequent death and resurrection of Jesus Christ. We could now possess *eternal life by God's grace*. The door had now been opened for us to attain true liberty: freedom from the shackles of sin and death. We could now fully realize our potential as those created in God's image.

Through Jesus Christ, God was making a way for reconciliation in the breach that had occurred from the time of Adam and Eve (see Genesis 3). That breach persists with human rebellion against God throughout the ages. But God was now providing an enduring solution in Jesus Christ for all the pain, sufferings, wars, conflicts, diseases, disorders and other misfortunes plaguing a fallen world. In Jesus Christ, we could now have complete victory over all human problems (spiritual, political, economic, personal or social).

Through Jesus Christ, we can have life, yes: the abundant life forever – praise God! Indeed, *the Son of God is the only door into the fullness of life, love, joy, freedom and peace available solely in God.* "For through Him we both have access by one Spirit to the Father" (Ephesians 2:18, NKJV; see also John 10:9 and John 14:6).

Joy through Love

God sent His Son to save us. He came to help us rise above the depravity and despondency that the human race has fallen into. Significantly, through Jesus Christ we learn of the power of the Holy Spirit to enable humans live according to God's commandments grounded in love. He showed us how to love God by loving people. That is, all peoples, no exceptions. Not discriminating, the Lord Jesus interacted with the poor, healing the sick and feeding multitudes.

At the core of God's commandments, *love is the key to enjoying the fullness of joy that the Lord offers.* And as Jesus noted while speaking to His early disciples:

"Just as the Father has loved Me, I have also loved you; abide in My love. If you keep My commandments, you will abide in My love; just as I have kept My Father's commandments and abide in His love. These things I have spoken to you so that My joy may be in you, and *that your joy may be made full.* This is My commandment, that you *love one another*, just as I have loved you" (John 15: 9-12, NASB, emphasis added).

When we love people, we are obeying God's commandments. That obedience brings joy. Loving others brings joy. So spread the love. Share the joy. Don't hold back please.

Names Recorded in Heaven

By operating in God's way of love, *helped by the Holy Spirit*, we indeed become joyful – praise God! A great benefit of our obedience to God is that He empowers us to overcome the challenges of this world. Those challenges include demons who can steal our joy. But by being aligned with God, we can resist and overcome them. The early disciples of Jesus Christ did just that. So too can you! In one example, the disciples reported to Jesus (after returning "with joy" from a trip): "Lord, even the demons are subject to us in Your name" (Luke 10:17, NKJV).

Jesus replied: "I was *watching Satan fall from heaven like lightning.* Behold, I have given you authority to tread on serpents and scorpions, and over all the power of the enemy, and nothing will injure you. Nevertheless do not rejoice in this, that the spirits are subject to you, but *rejoice that your names are recorded in heaven*" (Luke 10:18-20, NASB, emphasis added).

Jesus was focusing their attention on the most wonderful gift of all to humans: *eternal life with God* in the kingdom of heaven. Those with their names written in heaven get to spend eternity with God. It's a *joyous and pleasure-filled* experience that holds promises of wonders and beauty everlasting. For as King David wrote: "You will make known to me the path of life; In Your presence is fullness of joy; In Your right hand there are pleasures forever" (Psalm 16:11, NASB). Praise God!

Eternity with God *or* the Lake of Fire?

However, to spend eternity with God, there is one great hurdle to pass: the final judgment. Only those with their names written in the Book of Life will make it. While God's children *will not* suffer the second death, others will perish in the lake of fire (see Revelation 20:11-15).

In visions of future events when Jesus Christ returns, the apostle John wrote: "And I saw the dead, small and great, stand before God; and the books were opened: and another book was opened, which is the book of life: and the dead were judged out of those things which were written in the books, according to their works" (Revelation 20:12, KJV). "And if anyone's name was not found written in the book of life, he was thrown into the lake of fire" (Revelation 20:15, NASB).

Guarantee of Our Eternal Inheritance: the Holy Spirit

Those with their names written in heaven have a divine assurance. By God's grace, when Jesus Christ returns, believers will be part of the coming new world. As citizens of heaven, believers get to experience permanently, eternally its righteousness, peace, beauty, joy and harmony. And as joint heirs with the Christ, *believers get to inherit everything* (see Revelation 21:7 and Romans 8:17).

Our inheritance through Jesus Christ is guaranteed via the Holy Spirit: "In Him, you also, after listening to the message of truth, the gospel of your salvation – having also believed, you were sealed in Him with the Holy Spirit of promise, who is given as a pledge of our inheritance, with a view to the redemption of God's own possession, to the praise of His glory" (Ephesians 1:13-14, NASB).

Good or Bad Fruit?

Fundamentally, the Holy Spirit enables believers to be fruitful. We get to experience and demonstrate qualities, bear fruit that distinguishes children of God from others. Love and joy, indeed, are among the fruit of the Spirit as listed in Galatians 5:22-23 (NASB).

Under the power of the Holy Spirit, moreover, we are able to resist the ugly habits and deadly tendencies that can steal or destroy our joy. These are qualities or actions, bad fruit that counteract God's commandments grounded in love. You cannot inherit the kingdom of God with such bad habits or practices, as listed in Galatians 5:19-21. But by staying rooted in the Holy Spirit, believers can bear good fruit and inherit the kingdom of heaven with its everlasting joy.

Joyful in the Lord: Rejoicing in His Salvation

When Jesus Christ returns, believers will get a new spiritual, incorruptible body (see 1 Corinthians 15:42-58 and Philippians 3:20-21). Those saved will eventually be free from pain, sorrow and death (see Revelation 21:1-4). What a great relief – all praises to God!

"And my soul shall be joyful in the Lord: it shall rejoice in his salvation," so wrote King David (Psalm 35:9, KJV). You must be saved, however, to experience this great joy. So please make your peace with God now, *if you haven't already*. It's easy. Jesus has done all the heavy lifting for you. So why wait? Why miss the true, everlasting joy offered to you freely by God?

Don't delay. Please say this prayer now: *Dear God, please come into my life and help me to be joyful in the Lord: rejoicing in Your salvation. I acknowledge and repent of my sins and ask for Your forgiveness. I accept that Jesus Christ, my Lord and Savior, died for my sins and was resurrected by the power of the Holy Spirit. Please fill me up with the Holy Spirit so that I can live to do Your will. And use me for Your glory, for good works. In Jesus name I pray: Amen!*

Discussion Questions

1. Why is the gospel such good news of great joy?

2. What is the fullness of joy and how do believers get it? How is love related to that fullness of joy?

3. Who can benefit from this good news of great joy? And How?

Chapter 7

Born Again

Born Again: Rebirth into Eternity, a Fresh Start

Highlights:

- To enter the kingdom of heaven, you must be born again by the power of the Holy Spirit, giving you everlasting life (see John 3:16 and John 3:3-6).
- Rebirth into eternity is required because flesh and blood cannot inherit the kingdom of God which is perfect and holy.
- God loves you and desires for you to be born again, to get a fresh start for a new and better life that endures forever. You can leave behind your pains, sorrows, disappointments, hopelessness and helplessness forever.

Nicodemus came at night to see Jesus Christ. That encounter was illuminating. It was memorable, reverberating through time. "Most assuredly, I say to you," Jesus told Nicodemus, "unless one is born again, he cannot see the kingdom of God". What? Nicodemus, a Jewish ruler, was puzzled by what appeared to be a strange concept. You probably would have asked the same question he posed to Jesus: "How can a man be born when he is old? Can he enter a second time into his mother's womb and be born?"

"Most assuredly, I say to you," Jesus answered, "unless one is born of water and the Spirit, he cannot enter the kingdom of God. That which is born of the flesh is flesh, and that which is born of the Spirit is spirit" (John 3:3-6, NKJV; see also Ephesians 5:26). Essentially, by being born again, believers in God are given a rebirth into eternity (given everlasting life) through the transformational work of the Holy Spirit. Becoming citizens of heaven, believers won't suffer the second death, the permanent punishment for those who reject God's law grounded in love. Thankfully, believers have access to God forever in the kingdom of heaven. How awesome is that – praise God!

When Jesus Christ Returns

What then is the kingdom of heaven? Why would anyone desire to enter into it? At some point in the future when Jesus Christ returns, *God's kingdom will prevail completely. It will sweep away every spiritual, political, military, economic and societal power in the universe.* It will be the only realm standing in the coming new world. There will be a new heaven and a new earth, replacing the old as God comes to dwell among the saved (see Revelation 21:1-4, Isaiah 65:17, Isaiah 66:22 and 2 Peter 3:13).

Only those who are born again will make it. The rest will perish: "These will pay the penalty of eternal destruction, away from the presence of the Lord and from the glory of His power" (2 Thessalonians 1:9, NASB). Along with the devil and his followers, they will be cast into the lake of fire, which is the second death (Revelation 20:11-15). But believers will survive and flourish forever, enjoying a new spiritual, incorruptible body, with no more pain, sorrow, tears or death (see 1 Corinthians 15:42-58 and Revelation 21:1-4).

The Greatest Experience Ever

Those saved will come to dwell forever in the presence of a most loving God. Being in the same space as God is an experience that surpasses any other (see Psalm 16:11). If you have not made your peace with God, you will miss out on the greatest experience that is available to any human being. You can fix that tragic problem right now by taking your first step into eternity for the abundant life everlasting. Start by embracing God's righteousness through Jesus Christ today. Please make the right choice between life and death. Choose life.

Diseases, decay, death and destruction are part of the reality of this passing world. You don't have to end up like this doomed world, if you make the right choice. You can be among those redeemed to enjoy the new world with no more sorrows. "And God will wipe away every tear from their eyes; there shall be no more death, nor sorrow, nor crying. There shall be no more pain, for the former things have passed away," wrote the apostle John, speaking of the future (Revelation 21:4, NKJV).

Assuredly, those who are saved get to enjoy the endless benefits reserved only for those who are joint heirs with the Son of God. Why miss out on this great opportunity? God has made it possible through Jesus Christ for everyone to be born again, to gain eternal life (see John 3:14-16).

Flesh and Blood Cannot Inherit the Kingdom

Only those born again will experience the joys and pleasures that can be found in the presence of almighty God. In the new world, God will come to dwell with those saved (Revelation 21:3). To share in that experience, you must undergo a fundamental transformation, because "flesh and blood cannot inherit the kingdom of God; nor does corruption inherit incorruption" (1 Corinthians 15:50, NKJV).

That transformation occurs through the work and power of the Holy Spirit. It is the same power that raised Jesus Christ from the dead (also earlier enabling His human birth through a virgin, Mary). The atonement for sin by the Son of God provides an opportunity for us to escape the ultimate consequence of Adam's failure (see Genesis 3). Sadly, we have not done any better than the First Man. We've demonstrated *a startling human inability to rise above sin and its ultimate curse and consequence: death.* We need God's help.

The First Man Adam vs. the Second Man Jesus

Undoubtedly, the First Man Adam brought a curse upon us all (thereby corrupting, polluting the human race). Nevertheless, the Second Man Jesus brings a blessing for us all, for healing and rebirth. "The first man is from the earth, earthy; *the second man is from heaven.* As is the earthy, so also are those who are earthy; and as is the heavenly, so also are those who are heavenly. Just

46

as we have borne the image of the earthy, we will also bear the image of the heavenly" (1 Corinthians 15:47-49, NASB, emphasis added).

Believers in God (those saved) *eventually get to bear the image of the heavenly Man*, the last Adam: Jesus Christ. We ultimately inherit all of His incorruptible qualities for eternal life – praise God! "So also is the resurrection of the dead. It is sown a perishable *body*, it is raised an imperishable *body*; it is sown in dishonor, it is raised in glory; it is sown in weakness, it is raised in power; it is sown a natural body, it is raised a spiritual body. If there is a natural body, there is also a spiritual *body*. So also it is written, 'The first MAN, ADAM, BECAME A LIVING SOUL.' THE LAST ADAM *became* a life-giving spirit" (1 Corinthians 15:42-45, NASB).

Eternal Life, Faith in God and the Heavenly Man

To bear the image of the heavenly Man, to become born again, you must embrace the gospel of God through His Son Jesus Christ. It is the gospel of peace (Romans 10:15), of salvation into the kingdom of heaven. It brings through Jesus Christ redemption and regeneration for all who believe in Him.

"As Moses lifted up the serpent in the wilderness, even so must the Son of Man be lifted up; so that whoever believes will in Him have eternal life. For God so loved the world, that He gave His only begotten Son, that whoever believes in Him shall not perish, but have eternal life" (John 3:14-16, NASB).

Significantly, those who receive Jesus Christ, those who believe in Him, are essentially putting their faith in God. "Truly, truly, I say to you, he who *hears My word*, and *believes Him who sent Me, has eternal life,* and *does not come into judgment*, but has passed out of death into life" Jesus noted (John 5:24, NASB, emphasis added; see also John 14:1 and John 14:7-14).

Believers open themselves up to the transformational power of spiritual rebirth, passing "out of death" into a new life everlasting. "Therefore if anyone is in Christ, *he is* a new creature; the old things passed away; behold, new things have come" (2 Corinthians 5:17, NASB)! Praise God!

Sharing Sincere Love

In addition, as the apostle Peter wrote concerning those who are saved: "Since you have purified your souls in *obeying the truth through the Spirit in sincere love* of the brethren, *love one another fervently* with a pure heart, *having been born again*, not of corruptible seed but incorruptible, through the word of God which lives and abides forever..." (1 Peter 1:22-23, NKJV, emphasis added). Significantly, the Spirit enables you and me to obey God's greatest commandments to: (1) love God, and (2) love people.

You have the opportunity here and now to embrace God's way, if you haven't already. God's word will definitely come to pass, assuring you of salvation when you allow the Holy Spirit to work in your life. The Spirit empowers you, enabling you to become born again for eternity. If you haven't already done so, *take your first step into eternity now* for the abundant life everlasting. *Become born again.* Accept Jesus Christ into your life. Don't let the world deceive you with fake realities. There is only one reality: *you must be born again to survive and thrive into eternity.* God has made this privilege freely available to all through Jesus Christ – praise God!

You can be born again right now (if you are not saved). You too can access the kingdom of heaven and escape the wrath of God. Please say this short prayer now: *Dear Jesus, please come into my life. I want to be born again. I admit I am a sinner, and acknowledge that You died for my sins and was resurrected by the power of the Holy Spirit. I accept You as my Lord and Savior and pray that You fill me with the Holy Spirit so that I can live to do God's will. Amen!*

Discussion Questions

1. Why do we need to be born again and what does it mean exactly to be born again as Jesus Christ described it?

2. Can just anyone be born again – when and how can it happen? How is the Holy Spirit involved?

3. What does having a fresh start mean after you are born again – what does it translate into in practical terms?

Chapter 8

Forgiveness

Forgiveness: Guilty No More, Showing Others Mercy

Highlights:

- All humans owe a debt for sin payable by death: eternal condemnation with no escape from the second death – but the sins of those saved are forgiven through Jesus Christ.
- Those saved have eternal life, with the sin-debt paid fully at the cross and the blood of Jesus cleansing from all sin, cleansing the believer's conscience.
- Significantly, those desiring forgiveness from God are **required** to forgive others – if we forgive others, God forgives us.

A certain man owed his king so much money that he could not repay it. The king therefore "commanded him to be sold, along with his wife and children and all that he had". Pleading desperately, the debtor "fell *to the ground* and prostrated himself" before the king (Matthew 18:25-26, NASB). Moved, the king showed great compassion – he graciously forgave the huge debt. But the story, sadly, does not end there.

In a perverse twist, the same man who had just been forgiven found another man who owed him money. Showing no mercy and ignoring the other man's earnest pleas, the man threw the other in jail (Matthew 18:28-30). Distressed at this absurdity, witnesses reported the matter to the king who was furious, justifiably.

"You wicked slave, I forgave you all that debt because you pleaded with me," the king reminded the first man, as recorded in Matthew 18:32-33 (NASB). "Should you not also have had mercy on your fellow slave, in the same way that I had mercy on you?"

Required: Forgiving Others, Showing Mercy

Jesus, who was telling the story above, concluded: "And his lord, moved with anger, handed him over to the torturers until he should repay all that was owed him. My heavenly Father will also do the same to you, if each of you does not forgive his brother from your heart" (Matthew 18:34-35, NASB).

God, indeed, offers forgiveness for sin. But the Lord's forgiveness has a strict requirement. We all must forgive others as we are forgiven. We must show others mercy as we are shown mercy. "For if you forgive others for their transgressions, your heavenly Father will also forgive you. *But if you do not forgive others, then your Father will not forgive your transgressions,*" Jesus noted (Matthew 6:14-15, NASB, emphasis added).

If we forgive others, God forgives us. Without God forgiving us, we would remain guilty of sin, punishable by death: eternal condemnation. By being forgiven, we get to escape the wrath of God. Beyond that, moreover, when God forgives us, we get to enjoy forever His favor. We don't deserve it. But by God's grace, believers get access to tremendous benefits available to us because of the shed blood of Jesus Christ – praise God!

The Blood of Jesus Christ Cleanses from all Sin

"This is the message we have heard from Him and announce to you, that God is Light, and in Him there is no darkness at all. If we say that we have fellowship with Him and *yet* walk in the darkness, we lie and do not practice the truth; but if we walk in the Light as He Himself is in the Light, we have fellowship with one another, and *the blood of Jesus His Son cleanses us from all sin,*" the apostle John wrote many years ago (1 John 1:5-7, NASB, bold emphasis added).

Thankfully, our debt for sin is erased by the immense cleansing power of the blood of Jesus Christ. Forgiven by God, believers are guilty no more. We get relief from the consequences of sin. God frees us from the troubles of our defiled, corrupted consciences. What great blessings – thanks be to God! As King David wrote in Psalm 32:1 (NASB): "How blessed is he whose transgression is forgiven, Whose sin is covered"! Moreover: "Blessed is the man against whom the Lord counts no iniquity, and in whose spirit there is no deceit" (Psalm 32:2, ESV).

Everlasting Benefits and the Return of Jesus Christ

God's forgiveness opens up a wealth of endless blessings, everlasting benefits for believers. By God's grace, those saved (believers) are *propelled into a process* that eventually ensures our complete freedom from the curse and consequences of sin. The process culminates in the return of Jesus Christ, ushering in a new world in which God comes to dwell among those saved. Avoiding the second death, believers come to eventually live in the presence of a most loving, powerful, merciful and gracious God.

Our infinitely wise and merciful God has opened up the way for peace between the Creator and the created. Through Jesus Christ, salvation is freely available. "And as it is appointed for men to die once, but after this the judgment, so Christ was offered once to bear the sins of many. To those who eagerly wait for Him *He will appear a second time, apart from sin, for salvation*" (Hebrews 9:27-28, NKJV, emphasis added).

A Perfect Offering to God

By dying for our sins, *Jesus Christ was offering a better and everlasting solution* for humanity's greatest problems found in sin and death. We all have failed woefully to keep God's commandments perfectly, hence were all condemned to death. Out of love, God had to intervene to save us.

Overall, keeping God's commandments requires 100 percent perfection. You cannot make it into the kingdom of heaven with a lower score! "For whoever keeps the whole law but fails in one point has become accountable for all of it" (James 2:10, ESV). We humans are notoriously imperfect, unable to flawlessly keep God's law. So God had to provide a solution by Himself to save us from the consequences of sin.

Because God loves us and takes no pleasure in human destruction, *the solution had to fulfill the law (death)* **and** *give us eternal life (salvation)*. Humankind hence needed *a perfect and permanent atonement for sin found only in* **Jesus Christ**. In Him, the punishment for sin (death) is paid in full, bringing us salvation (eternal life) – praise God!

Since Jesus Christ was without sin, He died for sins He did not commit. By erasing our sin-debt, the Son of God provides eternal life to all believers in God. Through Him, the righteousness of God gets credited to our accounts. So, instead of death, believers get favor, eternal blessings – praise God! The depth of God's wisdom, His love, mercy and grace, in the salvation plan is beyond amazing. Thank You Lord for Your infinite love!

Significantly, the historical practice of animal sacrifice was inadequate to completely and permanently cleanse us from sin. "For if the blood of goats and bulls and the ashes of a heifer sprinkling those who have been defiled sanctify for the cleansing of the flesh, how much more will the blood of Christ, who through the eternal Spirit offered Himself without blemish to God, *cleanse your conscience from dead works* to serve the living God?" (Hebrews 9:13-14, NASB, emphasis added).

Cleansing of the Conscience

Notice the reference to the cleansing of the conscience in Hebrews 9:13-14 and compare it with Romans 2:14-16. Note also the reference to cleansing the flesh as distinct from the cleansing of the conscience. "…According to this arrangement, gifts and sacrifices are offered that cannot perfect the conscience of the worshiper" (Hebrews 9:9, ESV).

Only the blood of Jesus can cleanse the conscience. And it's a miraculous cleansing that is needed unavoidably. That is because a defiled, seared or tortured conscience is a troublesome burden. It steals one's peace, a dire consequence of sin. As God Himself declares in Isaiah 48:22: there is no peace for the wicked.

Note, moreover, that the old practice of animal sacrifice had to be repeated periodically. It was a temporary solution. But with Jesus, it is a done deal *forever* – praise God! "For the Law, since it has *only* a shadow of the good things to come *and* not the very form of things, **can never**, by the same sacrifices which they offer continually year by year, **make perfect those who draw near**. Otherwise, would they not have ceased to be offered, because the worshipers, having once been cleansed, would no longer have had consciousness of sins? But in those *sacrifices* there is a reminder of sins year by year. For it is impossible for the blood of bulls and goats to take away sins" (Hebrews 10:1-4, NASB, bold emphasis added).

But the blood of Jesus can take away our sins – praise God! It can cleanse us, *permanently* and *completely* – glory to God! The Lord Jesus is certainly able to "make perfect those who draw near". Jesus Christ indeed "is the mediator of a new covenant, so that those who are called may receive the promised eternal inheritance, since a death has occurred that redeems them from the transgressions committed under the first covenant" (Hebrews 9:15, ESV).

Favor: "the righteousness of God, through faith in Jesus Christ"

Through Jesus Christ, our sins are washed away forever and believers receive the righteousness of God. "But now the righteousness of God apart from the law is revealed, being *witnessed by the Law and the Prophets, even the righteousness of God, through faith in Jesus Christ*, to all and on all who believe. For there is no difference; *for all have sinned* and fall short of the glory of God" (Romans 3:21-23, NKJV, emphasis added).

There is no exception – all humans are guilty of sin. But God provides forgiveness through His Son Jesus Christ. So our salvation is strictly by God's grace. It's a gift. And with the Holy Spirit dwelling within us, thankfully, believers are empowered to obey God's commandments better than we could ever do on our own.

New Life: Bearing Fruit in Line with Repentance

Assuredly, God forgives our sins through Jesus Christ. We then must cooperate with the Holy Spirit, working within us to help us become better at loving people, to become better at forgiving others. This point is essential as a reminder so we don't mistake the righteousness of Jesus Christ as a cover to sin, to do harm to others!

In reality, we are to "bear fruit in keeping with repentance…" (Matthew 3:8, NASB; see also James 2:14-17 and Ephesians 2:10). We can show that we have *truly repented from a lifestyle of sin by demonstrating love,* showing compassion to others. We are to be fruitful in good works, showing the fruit of the Spirit. We must essentially reject evil works.

On the whole, for believers, God's forgiveness, when obtained, is complete. Our Heavenly Father does not hold back. "As far as the east is from the west, So far has He removed our transgressions from us" (Psalm 103:12, NASB). We get to start life all over on a new, clean slate: "This means that anyone who belongs to Christ has become a new person. The old life is gone; a new life has begun" (2 Corinthians 5:17, NLT). It is a new life founded on love. It involves showing others love as God has shown us love.

Love: "the bond of perfection"

Indeed, the new life require that we forgive others as the Lord forgives us, loving others as God loves us. Admittedly, forgiving others can be quite challenging. But God helps us. Through the Holy Spirit we are empowered to show others love, showing them compassion. We get to love them by forgiving their wrongs against us. We consequently get to avoid the fate of the first man in this chapter's introduction. Led by the Spirit, we are better able to make the attitude adjustment, the renewal of the mindset that forgiveness requires.

Undoubtedly, our ability to forgive others reflects how well we follow the teachings of Jesus Christ, the commandments of God, which are grounded in love. Besides, when we forgive others, we are actually doing ourselves a huge favor. Because we don't have to carry the burden of bearing grudges against others, our load is lightened by God's grace.

Clearly and conclusively, God has shown us how to forgive. After all, He gave us Jesus Christ *while we were still sinners* (see John 3:16 and Romans 5:8). As sinners, we were still at war with God in rebellion. Yet, God looked beyond all that and provided a way for reconciliation. As a result, we can get forgiveness, and beyond that blessings eternal: benefits immeasurable. That's favor from God! Praise the Lord!

As dear children, believers are to reflect God's forgiveness, His loving essence in perfection and holiness. And as Paul wrote: "Therefore, as the elect of God, holy and beloved, put on *tender mercies*, kindness, humility, meekness, longsuffering; bearing with one another, and *forgiving one another*, if anyone has a complaint against another; *even as Christ forgave you, so you also must do.* But above all these things *put on love, which is the bond of perfection*" (Colossians 3:12-14, NKJV, emphasis added; see also Romans 12:2 and 2 Corinthians 3:18).

Where is the Love?

Out of love, believers ought to share with others the good news of salvation. That includes sharing with friends and foes alike. It's about saving souls from eternal damnation. Do we not willingly share with others about where to get great deals on clothes, shoes and other things? Why not also share *the greatest gift and deal of all?* And yes, it's free. Absolutely free to us because *Jesus has paid the price – praise God!* Salvation is free to all who turn to God in repentance. It is however not available to those who reject God.

Seeing what a great gift God has given us through Jesus Christ, why should believers be quiet about it? Where is the love? Believers must not hold back. That involves showing others God's love through actions, not just words. It involves genuinely loving people as God commands us all to do. *Why stand by and let people perish forever?* Why not tell them of God's forgiveness available for even their most odious sins? Why not tell them of the good news of great joy?

There is definitely no shame in the gospel – believers are to share it freely under the direction of the Holy Spirit. For as Paul wrote: "For I am not ashamed of the gospel of Christ: for it is the power of God unto salvation to every one that believeth... For therein is the righteousness of God revealed from faith to faith: as it is written, The just shall live by faith" (Romans 1:16-17, KJV).

The gospel is the good news of how people can become reconciled to God, their sins no longer counted against them (see 2 Corinthians 5:18-21). Peace with God is possible. Forgiveness is available. Rebellion against God only breeds guilt, grief, turmoil, decay and death. It leads to a defiled, seared or tortured conscience. Those afflicted are denied peace forever. But salvation has come, thankfully, by God's grace. Salvation enables access to many great benefits in God.

So, please make your peace with God today, if you haven't already. And then be bold enough, as enabled by the Holy Spirit, to share God's love, telling others about this good news of redemption. Please accept God's forgiveness through Jesus Christ today. Say this prayer now: *"Dear Jesus, please come into my life. Forgive me all my sins. I acknowledge that You died for my sins and were raised from the dead by the Holy Spirit. I accept You as my Lord and Savior. Please fill me up with the Holy Spirit so that I can live to do God's will and share His love with others. And please help me to forgive others as I have been forgiven. Amen! Thank You Lord!"*

Discussion Questions

---

1. How can God forgive all your sins, even the ones people may consider too horrible? And how is the righteousness of God through faith in Jesus Christ related to the forgiveness of our sins?

2. What can or should you do to have your sins forgiven? And why should God's forgiveness of your sins not be taken as a license to commit even more sins? What do you understand from reading Ephesians 2:10, Matthew 3:8 and James 2:14-26? How can the Holy Spirit help you keep God's commandments?

3. Why is the cleansing of the conscience by the blood of Jesus so critical? And does being forgiven mean those who believe in God are now perfect and can sin no more? What is the implication of 1 John 1:8-10 here?

Chapter 9

Hope

Hope: Faith in God for a New and Better Life

Highlights:

- It is easy to give up hope in a world that is filled with so much pain, troubles and death.
- Those who put their faith in God however have hope and are assured of a new and better life: believers eventually get the perfect joyful life forever.
- Believers can look forward to the kingdom of heaven, filled with love, righteousness, peace and joy but freed from the problems of this world – praise God!

For Danny Velasco, this was the end. He checked himself into a hospital quite simply to die. He didn't want to die on the streets of New York City where he had lived homeless for a while as a heroin addict with hepatitis A, B and C. Hopeless, he had lost pretty much everything as a top make-up artist and now was about to lose his life – forever. His story, thankfully, doesn't end in the hospital, as recounted in the Brooklyn Tabernacle Choir's album titled *Live... This is Your House*.

Afflicted with phobias and fears while on the streets of New York City, Danny had been hearing disturbing voices. In the hospital, the voices continued to bother him, screaming and screaming in his head. But in all that cacophony, one day, a sweet voice broke through eventually. The voice told Danny he would become free if he called on the Lord's name. Danny then cried out with all his might, asking Jesus for help, telling the Lord He was his only hope. The Lord answered as He would to all who call on Him because "whosoever shall call on the name of the Lord shall be delivered..." (Joel 2:32, KJV; see also Romans 10:13).

Danny's Doubts about God Disappeared

The instant he cried out, Danny felt the Spirit of the living God sweep into his hospital room, overwhelming him, touching and healing him. Danny's doubts about God disappeared (he had not believed when a member of the choir had previously told him about Jesus Christ). That instant in the hospital, his phobias and fears all disappeared. So did the torturing voices. Praise God! Danny could feel the power of God's love and he knew immediately that God was real. Changed forever, he knew that God loved him and had heard him.

Surviving the hospital episode, Danny later became a member of the award-winning Brooklyn Tabernacle Choir. His story is a testament to the power of God to change lives and bring hope to the hopeless. *That hope in God for a new and better life is available to all today.* It is available to you now, if you are not saved! So cry out to God now just like Danny did.

Fresh Start: Many Benefits

Whatever you are going through today, know that God is able to change your situation for the better. *God loves you.* The Lord wants you to succeed in life forever. God can redeem you from all your troubles through His Son Jesus Christ, and give you a new, better and eternal life. Anyone therefore who is in Christ Jesus "*is* a new creature; the old things passed away; behold, new things have come" (2 Corinthians 5:17, NASB). Those saved get a fresh start for life, with access to many benefits in God – praise the Lord!

By following Jesus Christ, believers can trust in His great authority, supreme power as ordained by God. "All authority has been given to Me in heaven and on earth. Go therefore and make disciples of all the nations, baptizing them in the name of the Father and the Son and the Holy Spirit, teaching them to observe all that I commanded you; and lo, I am with you always, even to the end of the age," Jesus told his early disciples after His resurrection from the dead (Matthew 28:18-20, NASB).

A Winning Personality: Bright Outlook on Life

By aligning with this divine authority given to Jesus Christ by God, believers come under God's protective favor. Under this divine covering, we stand empowered, unmovable. By God's grace, believers can overcome the most difficult circumstances in this world. We reside, we move – yes, we revolve on a divine schedule, on an altitude of abundance. Indeed, believers get to navigate through life with an attitude of hope. It is a positive attitude that brightens our outlook on life. It helps us, by God's grace, to project a winning personality.

With God's loving help, believers can more ably stay elevated above the problems of this world. We don't drown in life's miseries, distresses and pessimisms. Instead, believers rise from height to height as we progress forward, soaring on divine hope. And by trusting in God, we hope to be among those who survive into the coming new world. Yes, by God's grace, believers will inherit the kingdom of heaven flowing in love, righteousness, joy and peace forever – praise God!

True Hope for Humankind

Only God's universal message of salvation offers true hope for a way out of the troubles confronting mankind. The human race remains under siege as times are getting tougher. Peace is a strange word in many parts of the world. Conflicts and wars persist. Mass murders continue as crimes abound, with disasters recurring in macabre routines.

Moreover, deadly diseases are unending, wreaking havoc ceaselessly, while hunger and want amongst plenty is a sad and continuous reality. Many have lost hope. Love is indeed a strange concept to many. Hatred has undeniably captured the hearts of multitudes, such that they cannot embrace this key injunction in the Holy Bible: "Owe nothing to anyone except to **love one another**; for he who loves his neighbor has fulfilled *the* law" (Romans 13:8, NASB, bold emphasis added).

Love and Light

Indeed: "Love does no harm to a neighbor; therefore love is the fulfillment of the law" (Romans 13:10, NKJV). *Those who seek to harm their neighbors walk in darkness, for they lack the light of God's love.* They lack hope. Sadly, doom is their end. They are condemned to stumbling through life, trapped in the darkness of sin, sorrows and death.

"The one who says he is in the Light and *yet* hates his brother is in the darkness until now. The one who loves his brother abides in the Light and there is no cause for stumbling in him. But the one who hates his brother is in the darkness and walks in the darkness, and does not know where he is going because the darkness has blinded his eyes" (1 John 2:9-11, NASB; see also 1 John 1:5-7).

Those not saved lack the illumination that lights the pathway to a brighter future and hope in God. Only frightful possibilities await this hopeless lot. Blinded by human ignorance and demonic deceptions, they traverse a darkened, despairing and hate-filled existence. They are filled with uncertainties and worries as to what holds in the next turn of events. Fear rules them. Phobias control them. Voices of confusion torture them. Death is their final chapter – for eternity. They have no hope, sadly, in God's salvation because they reject the Lord's way grounded in love.

Hope and Faith in God

But those who put their faith in God have hope through Jesus Christ. We have *the light of hope in God founded on love*, revealing the pathway to a brighter future forever. The Lord helps us. God charts a course through the chaos, dungeons, dangers and darkness of this world, giving us hope and much-needed protection as well as direction (see Ephesians 6:10-20, 2 Thessalonians 3:3, Nahum 1:7 and the chapters of this book titled: "Protection for Eternal Life" and "Purpose: Directions for Life").

And as noted in Psalm 27 (KJV):

"The Lord is my light and my salvation; whom shall I fear?
The Lord is the strength of my life; of whom shall I be afraid?

When the wicked, even mine enemies and my foes, came upon me to eat up my flesh, they stumbled and fell.

Though an host should encamp against me, my heart shall not fear: though war should rise against me, in this will I be confident.

One thing have I desired of the Lord, that will I seek after; that I may dwell in the house of the Lord all the days of my life, to behold the beauty of the Lord, and to enquire in his temple.

For in the time of trouble he shall hide me in his pavilion: in the secret of his tabernacle shall he hide me; he shall set me up upon a rock.

And now shall mine head be lifted up above mine enemies round about me: therefore will I offer in his tabernacle sacrifices of joy; I will sing, yea, I will sing praises unto the Lord".

Scriptures like those cited above help reinforce our hope and faith in God: "For whatever things were written before were written for our learning, that we *through the patience and comfort of the Scriptures might have hope*" (Romans 15:4, NKJV, emphasis added). Moreover, "hope does not disappoint, because the love of God has been poured out within our hearts through the Holy Spirit who was given to us" (Romans 5:5, NASB).

Furthermore, God "has given us the Spirit as a guarantee" (2 Corinthians 5:5, NKJV). Believers can trust in God for this divine Helper, enlightening us and strengthening our faith in God (see John 14:12-18 and the chapter "The Holy Spirit: Power, Love and Self-Control"). With the same Spirit that raised Jesus Christ from the dead empowering us, believers are assured of victory over all challenges in this world. We are assured of our inheritance in the kingdom of heaven forever – praise God!

Comfort and Directions for God's Children

Using the Holy Spirit, God provides comfort and directions for His children (see John 14:26). Through the travails of this world, the Lord strengthens us to **grow** *through* not just **go** *through* the hardships all humans must endure. God enables His children to survive and thrive in this fallen world, fortifying our character, hope and faith (see Romans 5:1-5). Believers can thrive despite adverse conditions because we have divine help and hope.

Unfortunately, those who are without God are stuck in the quicksand of futility. No matter how hard they try, their fate is failure, sorrow and death – the second death, for eternity, sadly. It doesn't have to be so because God has made salvation available to all.

Inevitably, this world will come to an end, ushering in a new world of peace and abundance under God's direct rule. To make it into the new world though, you must believe in God. It is a new world that believers look forward to: we get a new heavenly body (1 Corinthians 15:42-58). There will be no more pain, tears or death. Praise God!

Moreover, God will come to dwell with His children, providing light, sustenance and other great benefits. This is the hope for a brighter future that keeps believers going strong, waiting on the Lord and seeking first His kingdom and His righteousness. "The Lord is good to those who wait for Him, to the soul who seeks Him. It is good that one should hope and wait quietly for the salvation of the Lord" (Lamentations 3:25-26, NKJV).

New Strength and Better Life Forever

Furthermore: "Do you not know? Have you not heard? The Everlasting God, the LORD, THE CREATOR OF THE ENDS OF THE EARTH Does not become weary or tired. His understanding is inscrutable. He gives strength to the weary, And to *him who* lacks might He increases power. Though youths grow weary and tired, And vigorous young men stumble badly, Yet those who wait for the LORD Will gain new strength; They will mount up *with* wings like eagles, They will run and not get tired, They will walk and not become weary" (Isaiah 40:28-31, NASB; see also Jeremiah 29:11).

How should you respond to this knowledge about the one and only God who loves you? *If you are not saved,* know that God can give you hope to succeed over the travails and trials of this world. You don't have to be sad, pessimistic or depressed. You can have hope and a fresh start in life.

God wants you to be part of His family and share in His divine nature. You can be holy and perfect. Your life can be better. You can have a hope and a future in God who loves you. Victory over all your woes is assured with God's help. Life can be brighter for you. Why not become a child of God now?

If you are not aligned with God and His Son, you can fix that problem now. You too can get the new, better and brighter life in God forever. *Call out to God now like Danny did in that hospital room.* Danny had no one else to turn to for hope or help, but God. You have the same opportunity now if you are not saved.

Say this prayer now: *"Dear God, please help me and give me hope and peace. I confess and repent of my sins. I acknowledge that Jesus Christ died for me and rose from the dead by the power of the Holy Spirit. I pray that You please fill me now with the Holy Spirit so that I can have a better life and live to do Your will forever — in Jesus name I pray. Amen!"*

Discussion Questions

1. What does it mean to have hope and faith in God?

2. What is the hope that children of God have beyond this troubled and doomed world?

3. How can faith in God help people cope with the travails and trials of this world and become triumphant in the new age when Jesus returns?

Chapter 10

Purpose

Purpose: Directions for Life

Highlights:

- The path ahead of every human is filled with dangers – God provides the roadmap for us to navigate through the treacherous terrain of this world to emerge victorious forever.
- The roadmap God provides leads all the way to eternal life, because only God is able take us into eternity in the kingdom of heaven.
- And only God can reveal to us our true purpose in life – we need to connect with the Creator:
    - to learn why we are here on earth, and
    - to find the path to enduring fulfillment.

The delay seemed unnecessary. Chuck Swindoll's ship had stopped to wait for the harbor pilot in the waters of Formosa, today's Taiwan. Upon arrival, afterwards, the pilot proceeded carefully to steer the ship to the dock. The sailors then came to realize the reason for the wait. Death-traps lurked below. Mines were hidden in the waters, threatening instant disaster.

Just a little bump into one mine, and boom! The ship would have met a brutal end. Yet, the harbor pilot knew exactly where the mines were located, and skillfully navigated through the treacherous waters (see the book *Swindoll's Ultimate Book of Illustrations & Quotes* for more details).

The Minefields of Life and Light for Our Paths

So it is with life in general. There are mines everywhere. Without directions from the Divine Pilot who sees all things, we are doomed! We need His help. We need His ever watchful eyes to steer us away from hidden dangers and disasters. *We need Him to take us along the pathway that leads to the joy, peace, pleasures and prosperity of everlasting life in the kingdom of heaven.* This omniscient Pilot is the Heavenly Father: God, the Lord of heaven and earth!

With God, we have access to the ultimate in spiritual intelligence and power. We are therefore able to recognize and resist the masked horde of spiritual forces committed to evil. These are forces so evil, so cruel and powerful they can destroy anyone not under the Lord's protection.

Humans are not alone in this world – we have strong spiritual enemies! There is a devil who seeks our ruin. There are demons: they mean us harm. Additionally, there are multitudes of humans allied with the forces of evil. Outside of God's protection, we are dead meat before these nasty characters.

While giving purpose and meaning to our lives, God provides safety from evil. We just need to trust Him to help us find the right way through the maze, dangers and darkness of this passing world. "Trust in the Lord with all your heart, and lean not on your own understanding; in all your ways acknowledge Him, and He shall direct your paths" (Proverbs 3:5-6, NKJV). Indeed, God's "word is a lamp to my feet and a light to my path" (Psalm 119:105, ESV). Moreover, "I hold back my feet from every evil way, in order to keep your word" (Psalm 119:101, ESV).

Illuminating our path, God helps believers to navigate the minefields of this world. The Lord empowers us through the Holy Spirit. We are never alone, unaided. God's direction through the Holy Spirit is critical because He sees all and knows all. He knows where every road leads, and where every trap is set. He knows which paths lead to destruction and which pathway leads to the eternal, abundant life. *The Lord can steer us away from harm and towards blessings,* towards what we are designed for (that fits our purpose in life). We need God because He knows what is good for us, *what we are suited for.*

Good Works and Good Fruit

God's direction is so essential because He created us. He knows exactly what we are designed for. And He can give us what we need to become fulfilled in life, to fulfil our purpose in life. Without the Lord, we are lost and hopeless, headed for a ship-wreck.

For those saved (believers), God helps us to find our way. He gives us a guiding principle for success in life that applies to all humans. Grounded in love, the guiding principle entails that we *do good (and not harm) to others.* "For we are His workmanship, *created in Christ Jesus for good works*, which God prepared beforehand that we should walk in them" (Ephesians 2:10, NKJV, emphasis added).

Indeed, our primary purpose in life ultimately is to produce "good works" in all that we do – at work, at home, at school, or elsewhere – everywhere. That is what we are created for. *It **is** through these "good works" that we truly glorify God by bearing good fruit,* reflecting His very essence which is love. As Jesus told His early followers: "My Father is **glorified by this, that you bear much fruit**, and *so* prove to be My disciples" (John 15:8, NASB, bold emphasis added; see also Galatians 5:22-23, Matthew 5:16 and John 15:1-7).

God through the Holy Spirit empowers us to bear much fruit. As we submit ourselves more under the direction of the Holy Spirit, we can come to show more of the fruit of the Spirit: "love, joy, peace, longsuffering, gentleness, goodness, faith, Meekness, temperance..." (Galatians 5:22-23, KJV). By bearing much fruit, we demonstrate the power of God in transforming us to have the character traits needed to achieve our ordained purpose in life.

Significantly, our good fruit or "good works" are not in a vacuum. They are relationship based. They involve essentially *loving people, giving* – yes, giving of ourselves to serve others. We are to show God's love to others regardless of where we work, play or live.

We must avoid things that hurt people and focus on things that *encourage, help and build people up,* and not tear them down. It is through this purpose-driven life of showing "good works" to others that we can find lasting success and satisfaction. Such good works are at the core of God's purpose and meaning for our lives. Think of how much better this world would be if all humans were engaged in good works.

Light of the World

Believers have a huge obligation to bring the hope of God's love, God's salvation message to a dying world filled with so much sorrow and horror. Many people, unfortunately, are without hope and purpose. They lack love. They need God's guidance to find real meaning, deep value in their existence. Created in God's image, we all certainly do have great value, great worth to God. But human problems tend to taint that image in us.

So out of love, believers are to *point people to God*, to the kingdom of heaven: *the only hope of redemption from human problems*. We are to shine the light of God's gospel, God's love into a world darkened by hatred and self-centeredness. The light we shine should help people see their way out of the darkness, out of the wickedness of this world

"You are the light of the world. A city set on a hill cannot be hidden; nor does *anyone* light a lamp and put it under a basket, but on the lampstand, and it gives light to all who are in the house. *Let your light shine* before men in such a way that *they may see your good works,* and *glorify your Father* who is in heaven," Jesus told a multitude listening to His message (Matthew 5:14-16, NASB, emphasis added).

When we let our lights shine as children of God, illuminating people's pathway to the kingdom of heaven, believers are helping to change the world for the better. If more people are *focused on doing good works rather than evil works*, the world would certainly be a much better place. Many sadly have chosen evil works, so have contributed to the pollution, the ambiance of hatred that pervades and haunts the human race today. Failure is the inevitable outcome of such a dark pathway, such evil works.

Choices outside of God's will, outside of God's pathway grounded in love, only end in doom. Such choices take the route of selfishness and hatred, producing so much sorrows. It's the pathway of the proud, the way of the arrogant that God opposes because it lacks humility (see James 4:6). Because this evil pathway is the way of the damned, we are better off avoiding it.

Moreover, the devil and others will try to provide diversions to ensure that people miss God's way. So watch out – don't be fooled: "There is a way *that seems* right to a man, But its end *is* the way of death" (Proverbs 14:12, NKJV).

The Road to the Eternal, Perfect Life

God's way is better because it is built on love. It has the recipe for everlasting success. It shows how through love and faith in God we can overcome sin and death forever (see Galatians 5:6). In God's way, we can find permanent joy, peace and many other great benefits in God. Ensuring escape from the second death, God's way leads to eternal life. It provides access to the wonders and benefits of the coming new age (see the chapter "New World: No More Sorrow").

Believers get to inherit a new world free of the human problems we see today. It's a new world filled with everlasting love, joy, peace, beauty, prosperity and more. As children of God and joint heirs with Jesus Christ, we have eternal life. Believers get to partake of the divine nature, sharing in God's holiness and perfection forever – praise God!

Helpful Guide: Answers to Troubling Questions

In our journey on the road to eternal life, God is our ever-helpful Guide and Teacher as we continue to trust Him. From what I have seen in my life, the Lord is resourceful enough to foresee and address our doubts and questions along the way. This book, *Benefits in God,* is filled with answers to the many questions that others and I have asked about the issues of life.

Thank God for His illumination that has given me a better, reassuring and hopeful perspective on life! Praise the Lord! Indeed, God provides concrete answers to the many questions that may trouble us all, for instance: *Why do people die? Why is there suffering in this world? Why are people starving amidst plenty? What is my purpose in life? How can I fulfill that purpose? How can I overcome the obstacles to attaining that purpose?*

To all of the above and other questions, God helps us to find satisfying answers. As I have found personally in my life, God is the only One ultimately that can answer conclusively all of our troubling questions and erase our deepest fears. I remember one instance when I wondered within myself if there was another besides God. I didn't have a conversation with anyone about it. Just me thinking. Then one day, I was led to a passage in the Bible (see Isaiah 44:6-8 and 43:10-11). God's answer to my question was quite clear: **there is no other God**! Wow!

Prayerfully studying the Bible under the direction of the Holy Spirit is quite helpful in finding answers to our many questions. I know. I have benefitted from such Bible studies under the direction of the Holy Spirit – praise God! Studying the Bible helps us to stay focused on the right pathway to eternal life. Through it, God is able to redeem us from the discouraging doubts and darkness that our deep questions about the issues of life could bring. The Lord shines our pathway through the darkness so we can clearly see the divine blueprint for great, everlasting success.

As I have learnt, we *can get clarity when we ask for God's guidance, praying without ceasing and meditating on His Word.* We are therefore able to rise above the gloom of doubts and disbelief that plagues the human race today – praise God!

Our Roles and Goals

The clarity we get as children of God helps believers to know what roles we should be playing on earth. We all do have specific functions (see Romans 12:3-8). God doesn't leave us clueless about our roles and goals. In my experience, *God confirms for us what those functions are through the Holy Spirit, His Word in the Bible and through other believers.* (Caution: if someone gives you advice that contradicts the Bible, run for your life!) Moreover, God helps us in our daily decision-making processes *as we prayerfully seek Him.* He gives us the wisdom to navigate the dangerous terrain of this world as we interact with other people.

Because we are under His direction and protection as believers, no troubles or adversaries can bring us down permanently. Problems may come, but they only make us stronger (see Romans 5:1-5). They help reinforce our faith in God as we gain victory upon victory in our daily quest to do "good works". Because God is our Protector and Guide, we can go through our daily duties assured of our eternal security. Nothing, yes, nothing can prevent us from realizing our true purpose in life because we are being guided by the Divine Pilot, the Lord of heaven and earth – praise God!

Abundance for Eternal Joy

By God's grace, we will have an abundance in things good for everlasting joy. Our cups running over, we can be confident of God's provision for His vision concerning us as we walk in His purpose for our lives. And as King David wrote (Psalm 23, KJV):

"The Lord is my shepherd; I shall not want.

"He maketh me to lie down in green pastures: he leadeth me beside the still waters.

"He restoreth my soul: he leadeth me in the paths of righteousness for his name's sake.

"Yea, though I walk through the valley of the shadow of death, I will fear no evil: for thou art with me; thy rod and thy staff they comfort me.

"Thou preparest a table before me in the presence of mine enemies: thou anointest my head with oil; my cup runneth over.

"Surely goodness and mercy shall follow me all the days of my life: and I will dwell in the house of the Lord for ever."

Amen! Praise the Lord!

Discussion Questions

1. Why do you need purpose in life? What is wrong with just jaywalking through life?

2. How can you go about discovering what your purpose in life is from God? How is your purpose connected to doing "good works" and glorifying God?

3. What are the pitfalls or minefields on earth that God can give you directions and protection from?

Chapter 11

Rest

Rest from Your Burdens

Highlights:

- Life in this world can be troubling, discouraging and overwhelming.
- We all need relief, rest from the travails of surviving and thriving on planet earth.
- Divine help is available – we do not need to bear the burdens of this life alone, unaided by God.

Greg Laurie felt a profound change. "I had the distinct sensation that a tremendous weight had been lifted off my shoulder," he recalled of the day he accepted Jesus Christ into his life. A child of the fifties/sixties, Laurie grew up in the era of President J.F. Kennedy, the Beatles, Marilyn Monroe, Jimi Hendrix and other icons of that time. And then there was the Vietnam War. Like many of his generation, he looked to drugs for answers to the troubling questions that plagued him. And like any quest for solutions to human problems that ignores God, he only found emptiness and a sense of foreboding.

"I was told drugs would make me more aware, and in many ways that was true. I became more aware of how empty and lonely I was deep down inside myself," Laurie wrote in an *About Me* piece at blog.greglaurie.com. "After a particularly frightening drug-induced experience, I knew that I had to stop doing drugs forever." Besides, he had "seen the devastating effects of drugs on the lives of sixties cult heroes who self-destructed while still in their prime: Janis Joplin, Jimi Hendrix, Jim Morrison all gone".

Disillusioned, he had to contend with the 'Big Questions': "What is the meaning of life? Why am I here? And the one that really kept me up nights was, What will happen after I die?" It was only when he came to Jesus Christ that he found the answers to these questions and deliverance from his fears. Freed from the burdens that plague many today in this diseased world, he is now an evangelist spreading the gospel of God. Praise the Lord!

Like Greg Laurie, you too can find rest, relief from all of your burdens. The Son of God Jesus Christ is offering you genuine relief, real rest today: "Come to Me, all who are weary and heavy-laden, and I will give you rest" (Matthew 11:28, NASB). Life indeed lays heavy burdens on us all. We are barely able to bear them. People unfortunately tend to succumb under the heavy pressures, unable to get any type of rest or enjoy life to the fullest. It doesn't have to be that way. Whatever your problems are – no matter what your burdens or needs are – you will find their solutions and enduring fulfillment in God through Jesus Christ. "I am the bread of life," He says: "Whoever comes to me will never be hungry again. Whoever believes in me will never be thirsty" (John 6:35, NLT).

What do you hunger or thirst for in life? Peace, joy, love, happiness, prosperity or satisfaction? Or is it healing that you seek for some serious ailment, answers to disturbing questions, or relief from life's troubles? Is your life immobilized, minimized or undermined by all of these struggles? Do you want a better life, the abundant life, as God desires it for you? Do you seek the strength to thrive under your present situation and a future life free of pain, tears and death?

Then come to God now through Jesus Christ. The Son of God gave His life to atone for sin so that you can be nourished, enhanced and fulfilled in the joys of everlasting life. "For the bread of God is that which comes down out of heaven, and gives life to the world" (John 6:33, NASB).

A Divine Source of Aid

In the life that Jesus Christ is offering to you, there is rest from all your burdens. There is no need for you to keep suffering as if you are without a divine source of aid. It is okay to admit that you need God's help offered through His Son

Jesus. There is strength in recognizing your need for God. There is certainly no reason to keep looking for solace from your troubles in illicit sex, drugs, alcohol or other habits that only worsen your state of hopelessness. Your hope for redemption and solutions to all your problems can be found in God. "Oh, taste and see that the LORD *is* good; Blessed *is* the man *who* trusts in Him" (Psalm 34:8, NKJV).

But beware of false alternatives and fake solutions that can only get you deeper in trouble and make your burdens heavier. "There is a way *which seems* right to a man, But its end is the way of death" (Proverbs 14:12, NASB). The wrong ways to solve your problems may seem right at first, but in the end they lead to a dead-end of pain, regrets and death. As Greg Laurie found out, Jesus Christ is the best way, the only enduring solution for life's problems!

Moreover, as Jesus noted: "The thief comes only to steal and kill and destroy. I came that they may have life and have it abundantly" (John 10:10, ESV). Know the difference. Don't let anyone or anything steal, kill or destroy your potential for a divinely-ordained wonderful life. Accept the abundant life today, if you haven't already done so. Don't delay. Tomorrow is not guaranteed for anyone!

Life's Challenges: No More Failures

Trust in God to help you get through life's tremendous challenges. He can give you the internal fortitude to cope with your daily struggles. God can give you peace on the inside throughout life's numerous storms. He can enable you to see things on the bright side, to look beyond your present circumstances and to see that you have *many good reasons* to rejoice in a brighter future. But first, you need to ask the Lord to come into your life and help you, if you haven't already done so.

You need to accept God's salvation plan offered through Jesus Christ who died on the cross to bear our penalty for sin. His sacrifice provides redemption from the curse of sin which has caused so much havoc on us all. The consequences of sin span the failures in our personal lives, to problems in our socio-political systems, leading to an eventual dead-end in all of our endeavors. *Resolve today to be no more a part of the failures in this world.* Get out of the burden-filled, false and doomed lifestyle by embracing God now. "Cast your burden on the Lord, And He shall sustain you; He shall never permit the righteous to be moved" (Psalm 55:22, NKJV). Praise God!

Rest for Your Souls

There is no need for you to keep suffering when help is available. Answer your Maker's call today. Get relief from all your burdens now. The Son of God is calling you: "Take My yoke upon you and learn from Me, for I am gentle and humble in heart, and YOU WILL FIND REST FOR YOUR SOULS. For My yoke is easy and My burden is light" (Matthew 11:29-30, NASB). *Make the exchange today.* Why carry all that heavy stuff by yourself when the Son of God is offering assistance, enduring relief? He has paid the price for the transaction with His blood: there is no cost to you.

When you make the exchange, you take on the righteousness of Jesus Christ, who was sinless. You gain access to God's great powers, because the Holy Spirit that raised Jesus Christ from the dead will come to dwell inside of you. The Spirit empowers you to face life's difficult challenges today and secures your future in the kingdom of heaven for eternity. Take the Godly offer of help right now. Cry out to God in Jesus name now! Salvation is yours for the asking if you are not yet saved. Find rest in the Lord today!

Say this prayer now: *Dear God, please help me. I need the rest for my soul that Your Son offers. I accept Him as my Lord and Savior. I acknowledge and forsake my sins today. Thank You for Jesus Christ who died for my sins and was resurrected by the power of the Holy Spirit. Help me to do Your will from now on to eternity. Empower me to love others by Your Holy Spirit and spread the good news of salvation. In Jesus name I pray. Amen!*

Discussion Questions

1. Why is life filled with so much burdens for humans? Why can't we solve all of our problems, the ultimate of which is death, the ultimate killer, the demise of all that we may cherish?

2. How can God help us through the Holy Spirit to find rest from our burdens? How can the Lord redeem us from sin and death?

3. Why is Jesus Christ able to take over our burdens and how can we allow Him do it?

Chapter 12

Priority

Priority Number One: God – His Kingdom and His Righteousness

Highlights:

- Many issues contend for our attention daily, drawing us into things that can waste our precious time.
- It is very easy to become distracted from what really matters, to be diverted from rewards that can last forever.
- God gives us a focus on what really counts for eternity: the peace and joy of the kingdom of God and His righteousness centered in love.

"The kingdom of heaven is like a treasure hidden in the field, which a man found and hid *again*; and from joy over it he goes and sells all that he has and buys that field," Jesus told his early disciples, adding: "Again, the kingdom of heaven is like a merchant seeking fine pearls, and upon finding one pearl of great value, he went and sold all that he had and bought it" (Matthew 13:44-45, NASB). Jesus was illustrating the realignment of focus and priority that should come from us in response to the kingdom of God. Offering great treasures beyond measure, God's kingdom deserves our utmost priority, our primary focus.

With such a focus, we can concentrate *on what really matters in life*, yielding eternal rewards. It's a focus that *shields us from a troubled mindset tortured by worries*.

Hence we would no longer need to wonder "'What shall we eat?' or 'What shall we drink?' or 'What shall we wear?'" For God knows that we "need all these things" (Matthew 6:31-32, NKJV). Instead, our priority and focus must be to seek "first the kingdom of God and His righteousness, and all these things shall be added to" us (Matthew 6:33, NKJV).

Putting God First and Lacking in No Good Thing

When you make God your priority, you will lack in nothing good because "all these things will be added to you" (Matthew 6:33, NASB). And much more – praise God! You don't need to worry about anything as long as you trust God enough to put Him first in your life. "The young lions suffer want and hunger; but those who seek the Lord lack no good thing" (Psalm 34:10, ESV).

At the end of the day, you will *want your life to have counted for something,* fruitful for eternity. By focusing on God – His kingdom and His righteousness – you avoid the distractions that could condemn you to a wretched and wasted life. Caution: aiming for things that exclude God is dangerous.

You need to realize that God is the judge of the entire universe. You want what you do to count for eternity. You want how you are using the gifts and talents you are blessed with to be reckoned as worthwhile before your Maker. Created in God's image, we all do have something worthwhile to offer.

We are all responsible for how we spend our time, treasures and talents on earth. Wasting away your gifts from God on pointless pursuits is dangerous. When Jesus Christ returns, will you be able to stand justified at the Judgment? Will you escape the wrath of God against sin? Will you escape the second death? Will God give you great rewards?

Are you following God's law grounded in love? Have you put on the righteousness of God through Jesus Christ? Have you been engaging in good works or evil works? Will you be counted as guiltless or guilty of sin at the Judgment? Will you survive or be condemned forever?

The New Age of Love: Enduring for Eternity

Your answers will depend on your priority in life today. Do you have an eternity perspective? Are you seeking first the kingdom of God and His righteousness founded on love? Why? Simply because only God's kingdom will survive eventually.

In fact, the kingdom of heaven will permanently replace every social, economic, political or spiritual powers or entities that exist today. These have either failed, are failing, or will fail. The kingdoms of men, the realms run by humans, have been colossal, historical failures. So sad!

The present world is on a death march to ruin. It is passing away (1 John 2:17 and 1 Corinthians 7:31). Considering this sad fate, why focus on it? Why not make God, His kingdom and His righteousness, your number one focus? Why invest your passions and possessions on things that won't last?

When Jesus Christ returns to judge the world, a new age will be ushered in. By the grace of God, only believers will survive to inherit the new world free of pain, death or sorrows. All others will perish. Whatever treasures or investments they may have stored up for themselves on earth will not survive. Only treasures stored, invested in heaven can endure (see Matthew 6:19-21, and the chapter: "Prosperity: Riches in Jesus Christ, Rich toward God").

You too can have treasures stored in heaven, if you don't already. *You can get saved now, if you are not.* You can lock in your place for eternity in the kingdom of heaven today by God's grace! You too can be among those who will survive from this world. You too can be ushered into the kingdom of heaven for eternity *through the righteousness that comes from believing in and following Jesus Christ.* But your priorities must align with God first.

Producing the Fruit of the Kingdom

Speaking to a bunch of religious leaders who were insincere in their commitment to God and had their priorities mixed up, Jesus noted: "Therefore I say to you, the kingdom of God will be taken away from you and given to a people, *producing the fruit of it*" (Matthew 21:43, NASB, emphasis added). Moreover, as John the Baptist stated: "Bear fruit in keeping with repentance" (Matthew 3:8, ESV).

Love is a key element of that fruit. It is at the core of God's commandments (see Galatians 5:22-23 and Mark 12:31-34). Responding to a scribe who had wisely put the love of God and of people as the foremost commandments, Jesus told him: "You are not far from the kingdom of God" (Mark 12:34, NASB).

In addition, Galatians 5:19-21 describes the practices of those not producing the fruit of the Spirit who, as the apostle Paul warned, "will not inherit the kingdom of God" (Galatians 5:21, NASB). They lack love for God and for others. Therefore they are doomed.

Indeed, love is central to the fruit of the Spirit. Love makes it possible for God to forgive sin and grant access to His kingdom (see John 3:16). *When we reject love, we rebel against God and reject His kingdom.* That rejection is unfortunate because only God's kingdom will stand eventually. All other kingdoms, states or realms will fail and fall woefully forever.

The Great Reward for Loving Others

At the final judgment, how well we have demonstrated love to others, *doing good and not harm to other people*, will be greatly rewarded. "But when the Son of Man comes in His glory, and all the angels with Him, then He will sit on His glorious throne. All the nations will be gathered before Him; and He will separate them from one another, as the shepherd separates the sheep from the goats; and He will put the sheep on His right, and the goats on the left" (Matthew 25:31-33, NASB).

"Then the King will say to those on His right, 'Come, you who are blessed of My Father, *inherit the kingdom prepared for you from the foundation of the world.* For I was hungry, and you gave Me something to eat; I was thirsty, and you gave Me something to drink; I was a stranger, and you invited Me in; naked, and you clothed Me; I was sick, and you visited Me; I was in prison, and you came to Me'" (Matthew 25:34-36, NASB, emphasis added).

In addition: "Then the righteous will answer Him, 'Lord, when did we see You hungry, and feed You, or thirsty, and give You something to drink? And when did we see You a stranger, and invite You in, or naked, and clothe You? When did we see You sick, or in prison, and come to You?' The King will answer and say to them, '*Truly I say to you, to the extent that you did it to one of these brothers of Mine, even the least of them, you did it to Me*'" (Matthew 25:37-40, NASB, emphasis added: see also Matthew 25:41-46 for the fate of those who reject God's way of love).

An End to all Rule and all Authority and Power

When Jesus Christ returns, He will subdue all in this present world. "Then *comes* the end, when He delivers the kingdom to God the Father, **when He puts an end to all rule and all authority and power.** For He must reign till He has put all enemies under His feet. The last enemy *that* will be destroyed *is* death" (1 Corinthians 15:24-26, NKJV, bold emphasis added).

In the kingdom of God finally, death – the bane of mankind – would be no more! Sin would be no more. Love prevails. Only those saved will survive. God certainly wants everyone to be saved. He desires very much to give us all the treasures of heaven. Why not receive His everlasting gifts, His endless benefits today?

If you haven't, please start putting God first today. Make Him your number one priority now. Commit to embracing God's way, His commandments grounded in love now. Don't delay. You may not get another chance. Please say this prayer now: *Dear Jesus, please come into my life. And help me to make the kingdom of God and His righteousness my priority number one. I admit that I am a sinner, and acknowledge that You died for my sins and was resurrected by the power of the Holy Spirit. I accept You as the Lord of my life and pray that You fill me up with the Holy Spirit so that I can live to do God's will and enter the kingdom of heaven forever. Amen!*

Discussion Questions

1. What is the kingdom of God and how can you get into it? What qualities are connected with God's kingdom and His righteousness?

2. What is the righteousness of God and how can you obtain it and how is the fruit of the Spirit connected? What has love and good works got to do with it all?

3. What is your priority in life today? Is the fate of your life in eternity taken into consideration in picking that priority?

Chapter 13

Reconciliation

The Ministry of Reconciliation: Ambassadors of Christ

Highlights:

- Reconciliation with God brings believers into fellowship with the Creator.
- This reconciliation provides access for believers to all the blessings, all the benefits available only to the children of God.
- Reconciliation brings responsibility for believers to become ministers of reconciliation, ambassadors of Christ in proclaiming the gospel of God's kingdom to all.

When saved, we become reconciled to God, no longer at war with our Maker. In addition to the many benefits of being at peace with God, believers take on a new, exalted role. God elevates us to the status of His personal ambassadors to proclaim the message of reconciliation between God and humans in the gospel of Jesus Christ. "Now all *these* things are from God, who reconciled us to Himself through Christ and gave us the ministry of reconciliation" (2 Corinthians 5:18 NASB).

Ambassadors in the Line of Duty

It is a special ministry role that puts believers directly in the line of duty in God's work of salvation for humankind. What a privilege – praise God! As the apostle Paul wrote: "Therefore, *we are ambassadors for Christ*, as though God were making an appeal through us; we beg you on behalf of Christ, be reconciled to God. He made Him who knew no sin *to be* sin on our behalf, so that we might become the righteousness of God in Him (2 Corinthians 5:20-21, NASB, bold emphasis added).

As ministers of reconciliation, we get to work under the power of God. With the creator of the universe as our Helper, strengthening us, nothing is impossible as long as we walk in God's will, His way based on love. Desiring that none perish, God takes no pleasure in the destruction of anyone. So He equips believers to reach out to others and point them to God. He empowers us to have a mindset of reconciliation to do the work of ambassadors for the Prince of Peace, Jesus Christ.

A Mindset of Reconciliation

Admittedly, going about life with a mindset of reconciliation can be hard. There are people around who seem always ready to rub you the wrong way. Indeed, they can push your buttons, irritate you or even stab you in the back. What do you do then? The Bible recommends that you "bless those who curse you, and pray for those who spitefully use you" (Luke 6:28, NKJV). We are to be peacemakers, imparting grace even to those who come against us. "Blessed are the peacemakers: for they shall be called the children of God" (Matthew 5:9 KJV).

Fundamentally, believers are called to maintain a Godly composure that can help those attacking us come to see the light. In this vein, we are to "avoid foolish and ignorant disputes, knowing that they generate strife. And a servant of the Lord *must not quarrel* but *be gentle to all, able to teach, patient,* in *humility correcting* those who are in opposition, if God perhaps will *grant them repentance*, so that they may *know the truth*, and *that* they may *come to their senses and escape the snare of the devil,* having been taken captive by him to *do* his will" (2 Timothy 2:23-26 NKJV, bold emphasis added; see also Ephesians 4:29-32).

A mindset of reconciliation looks at the big picture. It entails a Godly response to contentious situations. Because God does not desire for anyone to perish, He equips His ministers of reconciliation, His *ambassadors of peace* with a helpful, positive mindset. It is a perspective that hopes for people to "know the truth". In knowing the truth that "they may come to their senses *and escape* the snare of the devil" whose captive they are.

Love: Forgiveness and Grace

It is certainly about *redeeming people from the clutches of evil*. Keeping that focus in mind can help believers become aligned with God's heart of *love, forgiveness and grace*. It is a focus that is critical to our function as ministers of reconciliation, ambassadors of Jesus Christ.

By operating in God's love, forgiveness and grace, we can become much better persons. Because God has forgiven us and shown us unmerited favor, believers must extend the same forgiveness and grace to others. As ministers of reconciliation, we help to make our environment a more loving, hopeful and healthy place to live in.

Believers are not to focus on seeking retribution against those who come against us. Rather, we are to be gracious to them, seeking their good and lovingly telling them about the goodness of God to humanity. We seek to walk in line with this injunction: "See that no one repays another with evil for evil, but always seek after that which is good for one another and for all people" (1 Thessalonians 5:15, NASB). If everyone in this world followed this injunction, imagine what a better place this world would be.

Discussion Questions

1. Why should we be reconciled to God? Was there a breach? When did that happen, what is our involvement and how can it be mended?

2. What does the ministry of reconciliation mean and why is it necessary? What is the role of the Holy Spirit in helping you become an effective ambassador of Christ?

3. How can we go about as ministers of reconciliation and ambassadors of Christ – what do we need? How can the Holy Spirit help us understand and practice 2 Timothy 2:23-26 and Ephesians 4:29-32?

Chapter 14

Success

Success by God's Grace

Highlights:

- Popular measures of success include money, status, property and power – but how accurate are these in truly measuring everlasting success?
- For success lasting forever in the abundance of God's kingdom, it is impossible to overlook the fate of the soul for eternity.
- Without your soul, without eternal life that comes only by God's grace, what success do you really have? Indeed, how can your soul survive without God's help?

Adolf Merckle was a billionaire. He had everything, or so it seemed. One day, unfortunately, he took his own life, according to a family statement (Dougherty, 2009). As reported by the *New York Times*, his body was found not far from his home in Blaubeuren, Germany.

The family statement, explaining why he did it, blamed the financial crisis affecting his firms along with uncertainties from the crisis. The situation had become too overwhelming for Merckle. He felt helpless. May God give his family the strength to cope with this great loss – I have experienced the passing of loved ones and I know how painful it can be. The cut is sharp and deep emotionally.

What Makes You Truly Successful?

Merckle's unfortunate end should provoke pause for thought, deep reevaluation of how we measure success. Does owning a lot of money (or things) truly make you successful? Does it bring you happiness, hope and peace? Does it help you cope with the distresses of life? What really is the greatest mark of success? Having a big house, a private jet, a luxurious yacht or your own island? Or is it being at the top of your career?

If none of the above, then what is it? What can outshine, even outlast all these and more? What can last forever? We find the answer in a simple question posed by the Son of God long ago: "For what profit is it to a man if he gains the whole world, and is himself destroyed or lost?" (Luke 9:25, NKJV).

Or to quote Mark 8:36 (NASB): "For what does it profit a man to gain the whole world, and forfeit his soul?" Gain your soul by God's grace in salvation and you get *everything* – you become eternally successful. Lose it and you have *nothing*. You forfeit yourself and become an eternal failure: that is the sad reality.

In the salvation offered by God through Jesus Christ, you get eternal life: your soul is secured forever. Because your name is written in the Book of Life, you escape the second death. By God's grace, you will not miss the new heaven and the new earth (see Revelation 21). Salvation guarantees you and me as believers a place in the kingdom of heaven forever. Believers are joint heirs with Jesus Christ, the King of kings.

Believers in God get to inherit a wonderful new world with great benefits in God. Know that this world is passing away (see 1 John 2:15-17). It is therefore dangerous to become attached to things that won't last, objects that don't provide everlasting success or satisfaction (see the chapter titled: "Satisfaction beyond Measure"). So be careful.

God Wants You to Succeed in Life, *Forever*

God wants you to succeed in life forever and not pass away with this world. The Lord gains nothing from your destruction (see Ezekiel 18:32). Neither do you. There is no *enduring* profit, gain or reward for those who put their faith in a world that is doomed to failure. Faith should be in God who is everlasting.

What if you don't make it into the coming new world? What if you are dead when Jesus Christ returns, *will you be resurrected into eternal life?* What will you have in the end if you perish, passing away with this world? Salvation from the coming doom is the key to genuine, everlasting success.

By being saved (your name written in the Book of Life), you are aligned with God. As a result, you get to attain the greatest status and privilege possible for any human being. You get to become a child of God, part of a royal priesthood (see 1 Peter 2:9-10). You become joint heirs with Jesus Christ, the Son of God. You get to be a citizen of heaven, partaking in the kingdom of God which endures forever – praise God!

In God, you get everything: status, wealth and power (superior spiritual power) – all the trappings of success in this world, and much more beyond this world. There is no success greater than that. By God's grace, you get eternal love, joy, peace and rest from all your burdens. Nothing can beat that.

God's Grace: Great Blessings

Fundamentally, God frees you from the clutches of sin and death, if you are saved. You don't have to pay for sin because Jesus Christ has paid it all. He took the hit for you and me. His sacrifice at the cross empowers us to reject and defeat sin, overcoming death – praise God!

By embracing God's way grounded in love, believers inherit along with Jesus Christ all that belongs to the Creator in a perfect new world (see Revelation 21, 1 Corinthians 15:42-58 and Romans 8:17). We get *the whole universe* (along with perfect new bodies) – praise God! There is no '*bling*' bigger than that, no blessings greater than that. And it all *comes only by God's grace.*

Neither you nor I deserve such great blessings from God, to be "heirs of God and fellow heirs with Christ" (Romans 8:17, ESV). But because of His unlimited love, God is offering us unmerited favor. "For by grace you have been saved through faith; and that not of yourselves, *it is* the gift of God; not as a result of works, so that no one may boast. For we are His workmanship, created in Christ Jesus for good works, which God prepared beforehand so that we would walk in them" (Ephesians 2:8-10, NASB; see also John 3:16). Praise the Lord!

Only the Best for Us: Wonderful Benefits Forever

God wants the best for us all. He doesn't want us to perish, but to have everlasting life (John 3:16). Although we were born into a sinful world and are ourselves immersed in sinful ways, God still sent His son to save us. The Lord sees our potentials and wants us to rise above the poverty of failures holding humanity back. God wants us to succeed. He wants us to overcome the helplessness and hopelessness of this world. God wants us to enjoy all His wonderful benefits, His endless blessings forever.

"For we also once were foolish ourselves, disobedient, deceived, enslaved to various lusts and pleasures, *spending our life in malice* and envy, hateful, *hating one another.* But when the kindness of God our Savior and *His* love for mankind appeared, *He saved us,* not on the basis of deeds which we have done in righteousness, but according to *His mercy,* by the *washing of regeneration* and *renewing by the Holy Spirit,* whom *He poured out upon us richly through Jesus Christ our Savior,* so that *being justified by His grace* we would be made heirs according to *the* hope of eternal life" (Titus 3:3-7, NASB, bold emphasis added). Praise God!

Success by the Renewing of Our Minds

The Holy Spirit, *"poured out upon us richly",* works out our rebirth into eternity. With the *"renewing by the Holy Spirit",* we become victorious over bad habits that could ruin our chances for everlasting success. Harmonization of our mindsets and actions with God's commandments is a sure outcome when the Spirit leads us. We are therefore empowered to avoid making the mistakes that have doomed many in this world to eternal failure.

The Spirit definitely reshapes our thinking. Our perspective on success, wealth, career, status and property changes for the better. We are transformed by the renewing of our minds to be more in tune with the Word of God (read more in Romans 12:1-3 and 1 John 2:14-18). We come to understand better why true success must include the fate of the soul for eternity.

The Principles of Successful Living

We come to understand, moreover, how following the principles of successful living outlined in the Holy Bible (grounded in love) can produce all-encompassing success always. Indeed, our success is not just for the future. The manifestations of God's grace on believers can be evident even right now, here on earth. Even in this doomed world – praise God!

Remember Joseph? Because of God's favor, His matchless grace, Joseph was successful in all that he did even in Potiphar's house where he was practically a slave. "The LORD WAS WITH JOSEPH, so *he became a successful man*. And he was in the house of his master, the Egyptian. Now his master saw that the LORD WAS WITH HIM AND *how* the LORD CAUSED ALL THAT HE DID TO PROSPER IN HIS HAND" (Genesis 39:2-3, NASB, bold emphasis added).

And as King David recorded in Psalm 1:1-3 (KJV, emphasis added):

> "Blessed is the man that walketh not in the counsel of the ungodly, nor standeth in the way of sinners, nor sitteth in the seat of the scornful. *But his delight is in the law of the Lord; and in his law doth he meditate day and night.* And he shall be like a tree planted by the rivers of water, that bringeth forth his fruit in his season; his leaf also shall not wither; and whatsoever he doeth shall prosper" (see also Matthew 22:37-40 and Romans 13:9-10).

Significantly, a *lifestyle of delighting ourselves in God's law grounded in love is at the heart of successful living.* When God is with you and me, when we delight in His law, our success is guaranteed forever. Whatever we do therefore "shall prosper". We get to prosper despite all obstacles for now and eternity – praise God!

Additionally, as God told Joshua: "This Book of the Law shall not depart from your mouth, but you *shall meditate on it day and night, so that you may be careful to do according to all that is written in it.* For then you will make your way prosperous, and *then you will have good success.* Have I not commanded you? Be strong and courageous. Do not be frightened, and do not be dismayed, for *the Lord your God is with you wherever you go*" (Joshua 1:8-9, ESV, emphasis added). Amen!

Moreover, when temptation comes, as it did to Joseph, we *must remain steadfast in God's way.* And quickly repent when we do fall into sin (see 1 John 1:7-10), endeavoring to avoid further comprise by worldly distractions. Indeed, with the help of the Holy Spirit, we can stay focused on the kingdom of heaven and live by Godly principles successfully. Praise God!

We are therefore better able, for instance, to avoid coveting the things in this world that can divert us from God. And when trials come with tough conditions, we can respond by God's grace like the apostle Paul did with confidence and contentment (Philippians 4:11-12). No matter what happens, or the situation we find ourselves in, we will be successful in doing God's will by God's grace. Amen!

Giving Back: Loving People – Sharing the Good News

As children of God, believers do have a unique view of success that focuses on eternity, eternal life. Our success goes beyond the here and now. We have one objective in mind: that is, to be rich toward God as we daily seek first His kingdom and His righteousness (see the chapter "Prosperity: Riches in Jesus Christ, Rich toward God"). That means an unshakable commitment to loving people, helping people. God expects us especially to help the poor (see Matthew 19:21).

Significantly, it is critical that believers show and share God's love by helping people come to Jesus Christ. Helping people without pointing them to *the Son of God Jesus* can leave them hopeless ultimately. Their salvation cannot be ignored. Believers in God must therefore *share the good news of great joy, as well as our worldly fortunes, with others.*

Fundamentally, our generosity to others acknowledges a key precept: whatever we have, we have received from God anyway. If it's wealth, for instance, we owe it all to God. "But you shall remember the LORD your God, for it is He who is giving you power to make wealth..." (Deuteronomy 8:18, NASB).

Furthermore, as Paul asked in 1 Corinthians 4:7 (NKJV): "For who makes you differ *from another?* And what do you have that you did not receive? Now if you did indeed receive *it,* why do you boast as if you had not received *it?*"

So, there is really no reason or room for arrogance because *God made us and gave us what we have.* The Lord gave us the innate faculties and the earthly resources that we use to create wealth or to get ahead, so why not give back? Why not share God's blessings with others? Why not love others as God commands us to do? Why conceal the good news of salvation from others?

Making the World Better

By giving back, we are making the world a better place. We are countering a diseased culture that operates on a misguided notion of success. It is a notion that thrives on the erroneous premise that to get ahead we must step on other people, taking from them and hurting them. It is a notion tied to a misperception in this world that acquiring worldly wealth (money, power, status or property) is the ultimate mark of success, regardless of its means of acquisition. But the pursuit of wealth, property or status *without regard for God* can lead to unnecessary grief and eternal failure. So be careful.

Aiming for the Top

When we aim for worldly wealth, for instance, or to reach the top in our various fields of endeavors, it must be under Godly principles. In fact, many of God's children are blessed with great wealth or achievements in this life – praise God!

The difference is that, for a child of God with say billions or status and power, the achievement is not the focus. It is *not* the number one priority – the focus is on God's kingdom and His righteousness. *Wealth or achievement is just one more means to love people and help spread the gospel of salvation.* It is for the believer a means to do God's will, otherwise it is useless, and cannot bring lasting success.

Sadly, many people regard acquiring a lot of money (regardless of who gets hurt in the process) as the ultimate mark of success. Beware: there is danger in becoming attached to worldly achievements or developing a love for money (see 1 Timothy 6:10-11). God and people, *not* money, should be the object of our love (see Matthew 6:24, Leviticus 19:17-18 and Matthew 22:37-40).

A Focus on Loving People

We are to *love people, not hurt them.* Embracing this perspective as a lifestyle is indeed *the essence of successful living.* We must hence flee the things that can cause us to stray from faith in God, from *delighting in God's law grounded in love.* We are to focus on doing good works. We must therefore avoid evil works. We must avoid the things that can turn our hearts cold towards other humans.

The greediness, for instance, that the love of money brings is dangerous. Greedy people tend to hurt other people. They don't care who gets hurt in their pursuit of career, status, property or wealth. They don't have a regard for God. They don't care about investing in heaven, storing their treasures where it is secured for ever – because they don't believe in it.

For the lovers of money, their hearts are tied to inanimate, heartless objects. These are objects that have taken the place of God in their lives (idol worship is still very much alive today sadly). Their hearts are lost in things that cannot love them back. God loves you. Money doesn't. Money can be a cold, heartless master: here today, gone tomorrow. But God endures forever!

Only God loves you to the point of giving His Son's life to save your soul. Only God can give you eternal wealth and success. So, why invest in any other? If you haven't already done so, please embrace the gift of God through Jesus Christ today. Don't invest in things that won't last forever. Don't ignore eternal life. Come to God now! Don't delay. Come to the way of everlasting success.

Embrace now the success that comes only by God's grace. Please say this prayer now: *Dear God, please help me! Give me true, everlasting success. I want to avoid making the mistakes that have doomed this world. Thank You for sending Jesus Christ, my Lord and Savior, to die for my sins. Thank You for His resurrection which gives me hope for eternal life in abundance. I acknowledge my sins and repent of them, and ask You by the power of the Holy Spirit to come into my life and enable me to do Your will. In Jesus name I pray, Amen!*

Reference

- Dougherty, C. (2009). Facing Losses, Billionaire Takes His Own Life. *The New York Times*. Retrieved from http://www.nytimes.com/2009/01/07/business/worldbusiness/07merckle.html?_r=0

Discussion Questions

1. What is the greatest mark of success? How can you gain it by God's grace?

2. How is delighting yourself in God's law and meditating on it related to the principles of successful living? What has loving your neighbor got to do with it all – specifically, how is applying God's law profitable for successful living?

3. What are your most valuable possessions: *did your soul make the top of the list?* Why is preserving your soul so important? What is the alternative and how can you avoid it?

Chapter 15

Confidence

Confidence: Favored for Greatness *and* Godliness

Highlights:

* Being aligned with God gives the believer tremendous confidence to face seemingly insurmountable challenges.
* No matter how big or bad our problems may appear, God offers us the pathway to overcoming them all.
* Our faith, our confidence in God's power inspires us to heights of greatness that can bring great blessings to other human beings.

The giant came spoiling for a fight. No one dared to meet him in battle. As the opposing army cowered in fear, a brave shepherd boy stepped up to meet the challenge. Confident of his strength in God, the boy told his king: "Your servant has killed both lion and bear and this uncircumcised Philistine will be like one of them, seeing he has defied the armies of the living God" (1 Samuel 17:36, NKJV).

After picking his preferred weapons – five stones and a sling (1 Samuel 17:40) – staff in hand, the boy approached the enemy. The giant was unimpressed: "Am I a dog, that you come to me with sticks?" He taunted the boy: "Come to me, and I will give your flesh to the birds of the sky and the beasts of the field" (1 Samuel 17:43-44, NASB).

Emboldened by his faith in God, the boy was unfazed. "You come to me with a sword, with a spear, and with a javelin," he told the giant. "But I come to you in the name of the LORD of hosts, the God of the armies of Israel, whom you have defied…. the LORD does not save with sword and spear; for the battle *is* the LORD's, and He will give you into our hands" (1 Samuel 17:45-47, NKJV).

In the face-off that followed, the boy David defeated the giant Goliath. By God's grace, he did it with a well-aimed sling-shot. Definitely, as David has shown (and *so can you*), Godly confidence enables anyone, even a shepherd boy, to knock down the giants of this world!

A Great King

That bold boy later became a great king in Israel. Moreover, it is through his lineage that the Messiah would later come, that is, Jesus Christ our Lord, making God's salvation possible for everyone. As a result, even someone like me (and you), by God's grace, can make it into the kingdom of heaven – praise God!

As children of God, we have unstoppable confidence. Through the power of God in Jesus Christ, believers can do all things (see Philippians 4:13), within God's will, of course (see also Romans 8:28). Our victory is assured ultimately over all obstacles. That is, as long as we are led by the Holy Spirit (see Romans 8:14 and Galatians 5:16-23).

Through the Holy Spirit, dwelling within us as children of God, believers are empowered to walk in God's way grounded in love. We walk in the confidence of God's power, not trusting in human strength. "For we are the circumcision, who worship God in the Spirit, rejoice in Jesus Christ, and have no confidence in the flesh" (Philippians 3:3, NKJV; see also Isaiah 2:22 and Psalm 146:3-10). Know this: human power, without God, will eventually fail you. But in God our triumph is everlasting – praise God!

Confidence in God

Our confidence is in God hence. It is a confidence that emboldens believers to do what is right regardless of the dangers because we trust in the Lord's power, protection and provision. "Trust in the LORD AND DO GOOD; Dwell in the land and cultivate faithfulness. *Delight yourself in the LORD; And He will give you the desires of your heart*" (Psalm 37:3-4, NASB, emphasis added).

For those of us seeking God, we shall "lack no good thing" (Psalm 34:10, ESV), as we engage in doing good works (see Ephesians 2:10 and 1 Timothy 6:17-19). We are assured that when we obey God, He not only gives us the desires of our hearts, but also handles the consequences of our obedience.

As the great preacher Charles Stanley would say in his sermons: *Obey God and leave all the consequences to Him.* Daniel did just that in Babylon, for instance, and God ensured that his needs were met. No one could harm Daniel: God gave him victory over all his adversaries.

People may conspire to bring you down out of jealousy for where God has elevated you to. But like Daniel, as a believer, be confident that God can protect and sustain you. The key is to *maintain your integrity in God* regardless of the changing times or shifting conditions.

Daniel: Believing, Trusting and Obeying God

During Daniel's lifetime, conditions did change. God nevertheless sustained him as he stayed steadfast in believing, trusting and obeying God. Do you know how Daniel rose to prominence even as a captive in Babylon? He had resolved not to be like many of his countrymen. They had been overthrown for walking away from God. They had lost their lands and were swept away into captivity sadly.

But Daniel sought to *live by Godly standards* (Daniel 1). Moreover, he acknowledged the sins of his countrymen: they had rejected God's commandments (Daniel 9). Daniel sought to do better and God noticed him. In fact, God notices anyone who seeks to do right. *"The Lord looks down from heaven upon the children of men, To see if there are any who understand, who seek God"* (Psalm 14:2, NKJV, emphasis added).

So Daniel was in a good place, *positioned for favor from God.* And when King Nebuchadnezzar of Babylon had a dream that no one else could interpret, Daniel prayed to God along with his friends. God responded with the interpretation (Daniel 2).

If Daniel had not been seeking to live by God's commandments, his story would have ended differently. But he got promoted. So will you too, by God's grace, when your confidence is in God like Daniel. He became "ruler over the whole province of Babylon, and chief administrator over all the wise men of Babylon" (Daniel 2:48, NKJV). *More importantly, at the end of the age, Daniel gets his everlasting inheritance* (Daniel 12:13). So will you too if you are saved – praise God!

Confident on the Day of Judgment

By God's grace, Daniel even went on to write great prophesies about future events in the world (read the whole book of Daniel in the Holy Bible). In the end, like other children of God who have died, he is assured of being resurrected to get his inheritance.

By atoning for our sins, Jesus Christ has paved the way into eternity for Daniel and the rest of us who have faith in God. *We can stand confident on the Day of Judgment (1 John 4:17).* By God's grace, believers get to inherit the coming new world full of God's best, blessings and benefits but free from pain, tears, sin and death.

Undoubtedly, as Daniel's rise in Babylon demonstrates, *faith in God can yield great benefits.* That faith is based on confidence in God's supreme power over all – everything, every being. God can take you from the lowest valley to the highest pinnacle and give you eternal life. That is, as long as you accept Him as the Lord of your life as Daniel, David, Joseph and many others did, and are doing.

You too can have that confidence in God – that is, if you don't already have the assurance of God's everlasting provision in your life. All the blessings from God can be yours if you cry out to the Lord for help. It doesn't have to be a complicated prayer. You can simply and sincerely right now say: ***Please Lord help me!*** God will take care of the rest.

Unwavering Confidence

In time, as the story of Daniel unfolds, when another king came to power in the land, God continued to bless him. The new king made Daniel one among three 'super' governors (Daniel 6:1-2). Yet, people sought to bring Daniel down. They deceived the king into signing a law, making it such "that whoever petitions any god or man for thirty days" except the king "shall be cast into the den of lions" (Daniel 6:7, NKJV).

But Daniel did not budge. *He kept on praying to God as usual.* So should you and I under similar conditions. Daniel persisted in trusting the one true God despite being thrown into the lion's den. And God saved him – praise the Lord!

Remarkably, Daniel's confidence in God stayed unwavering – remarkable, because to others, his actions may have seemed stupid. But he had a different mindset. *An earth-bound mindset would have been frightened into compromise. But Daniel was looking to heaven.* As a result, he survived the lion's den by God's grace.

"My God sent His angel and shut the lions' mouths, so that they have not hurt me, because I was found innocent before Him; and also, O king, I have done no wrong before you," Daniel told King Darius afterwards (Daniel 6:22, NKJV). Those who sought his ruin ended up food for the lions!

Confidence and Strength – Victory over all Adversities

As the stories of Daniel and others illustrate, there is victory over adversity for all who maintain their confidence, trust and integrity in God. The story of Joseph in Egypt especially is one you should check out as well – his faithfulness to God is similar to Daniel's (see Genesis 37-45).

Indeed, all these stories of confidence in God producing great successes prove that *you don't have to compromise your integrity to survive or flourish.* And it doesn't matter if you are in politics, business or any other sphere of human endeavor. God is able to sustain and elevate you – praise God! No enemy or circumstance is too big for the Lord to handle or overcome.

By God's grace today, if you are a believer, you can rely boldly on these words, and praise God continually for your victory: "*No weapon that is formed against thee shall prosper*; and every tongue that shall rise against thee in judgment thou shalt condemn. This is the heritage of the servants of the LORD, and their righteousness is of me, saith the LORD" (Isaiah 54:17, KJV, emphasis added; see also Psalm 34:19). Our victory is assured forever because our God is greater than all and loves us deeply.

Indeed, nothing can separate us from God's love: "For I am persuaded, that neither death, nor life, nor angels, nor principalities, nor powers, nor things present, nor things to come, Nor height, nor depth, nor any other creature, shall be able to separate us from the love of God, which is in Christ Jesus our Lord," wrote the apostle Paul many years ago (Romans 8:38-39, KJV).

This is the confidence that the children of God possess: that no matter what may come against us, we will prevail. No matter how many people plot against us, they will fail. No matter how high or powerful are the spiritual forces of evil arrayed against us, we will win by God's grace.

We can remain victorious because we stay confident and strong in the Lord. "For thus says the Lord God, the Holy One of Israel: 'In returning and rest you shall be saved; in quietness and confidence shall be your strength…'" (Isaiah 30:15, NKJV). Like David, Daniel and Joseph, you too should put your hope, trust and confidence in God. Please do it today, if you haven't already. I pray that you do, in Jesus name – amen!

Please say this prayer now, if you are not yet a believer in God: *Dear God, please help me. I repent of my sins and accept the sacrifice on the cross by Jesus Christ who died for my sins. I accept Jesus Christ as my Lord and Savior. I believe the Holy Spirit raised Him up from the dead and I have confidence in You for eternal life. Please fill me up with the Holy Spirit so that I can live to do Your will in complete confidence, faith and truth. In Jesus name I pray, amen!*

Discussion Question

1. Why was David so bold and not afraid of Goliath? How did his earlier victories over the bear and the lion affect his confidence level? How does Romans 5:3-5 relate here?

2. How can you obtain the steadfast confidence in God that Daniel had to know that you will ultimately prevail by continuing to obey God regardless of the challenges or oppositions?

3. What must you do to position yourself in righteousness so that God favors you, with His vast powers working to help you?

Chapter 16

Knowledge

The Knowledge of God

Highlights:

- To know God is to know yourself because you are created in God's image – God is love: therefore when you love, you are behaving more like God.
- But when you walk outside of love, you're operating in a mode outside of God's way – the result is sin which brings sorrows, decay and death.
- And when you know God, you are able to model yourself after the Original to fully realize your potential in love, perfection and holiness as exemplified by the Son of God.

Who is God? Does He even exist? If so, where can I find Him? How can I know Him? Does He love me? For these and other questions about God, the path to finding answers can start with a simple, sincere call. "The Lord is near to all who call upon Him, To all who call upon Him in truth" (Psalm 145:18, NASB). If you reach out truly seeking God, you *will* find Him. And when you do find Him, and become saved, you will discover the truth about yourself and become free to possess all that you'll ever need forever!

From my personal experience, I can say with great confidence that in seeking the truth about God, it's best to come at it with an open mindset. *Come wholeheartedly and sincerely.* God will take care of the rest because *He wants YOU to know HIM.* But the fakers – those not sincere about seeking the truth – are doomed to missing it. They end up deceived, sadly.

A Heart Steeped in Love

Speaking through the Prophet Jeremiah, God told the ancient nation of Israel: "For I know the thoughts that I think toward you, says the Lord, thoughts of peace and not of evil, to give you a future and a hope. Then you will call upon Me and go and pray to Me, and I will listen to you. And you will seek Me and find Me, *when you search for Me with all your heart*" (Jeremiah 29:11-13, NKJV, emphasis added).

The message above sent through Jeremiah contains an example that all in mankind can follow. God was indicating how to seek Him. The search *must be whole-hearted, not half-hearted.* No games! Be sincere, or you will find nothing. *Go at it with all you've got and stay open.* And you will come to know the heart of God, a heart steeped in love.

In getting to know the Creator, you will discover His intentions towards us all. His thoughts towards us are of love. They are of peace and not evil, assuring our eternal future in the hope and freedom of salvation through Jesus Christ. Ultimately, God seeks to mold us in the image of His Son so that we can come to truly realize our full potential.

Reflecting God in Love

To realize our full potential, essentially, we must reflect God as exemplified in His Son Jesus Christ. Because we are created in God's image, the process of seeking God and self-discovery can reveal how well we reflect or reject God. And we reflect or reject God *by how well we reflect or reject love.* Yes, love, because God *is* love!

For me personally, one of the most striking revelations about God has been this line from the Holy Bible: "The one *who does not love does not know God*, for God is love." (1 John 4:8, NASB, emphasis added). In effect, to know God is *to love!* Jesus Christ Himself emphasized the importance of love when He stated the greatest commandments from God to be: *to love God* **and** *to love people* (Mark 12:28-34; see also Matthew 22:37-40).

Love heals and helps people. Love is about giving to others, not taking or stealing from them. Love is certainly not about hurting people. That is because when we harm people, we break the commandments of God, and make the world a horrible place for everybody.

Romans 13:9-10 (NKJV) captures the essence of what that love translates into in practical terms: "For the commandments, 'You shall not commit adultery,' 'You shall not murder,' 'You shall not steal,' 'You shall not bear false witness,' 'You shall not covet,' and if *there is* any other commandment, are *all* summed up in this saying, namely, 'You shall love your neighbor as yourself.' Love does no harm to a neighbor; therefore love *is* the fulfillment of the law".

Mirror Watch: Self-Discovery and God's Image

Indeed, one of the most exciting aspects of getting to know the truth about God is that you get to know yourself better, even if in contrast. "We cannot know ourselves truly unless we know our God truly," says author Norman Geisler in a presentation titled *The Importance of Knowing the True God*. Geisler adds: "The best way to know humans made in God's image is to know God in whose image they are made".

Most definitely, it is from learning about the Original (God) that you can surely come to more fully understand the copy (humans). And it is in understanding how the copy has been damaged and can be mended, that you can better appreciate why humans need help. *The damage comes from sin and the solution lies in salvation by God's grace through His Son Jesus Christ* – praise God!

Aspiring to a Higher Standard

Knowing the Original, moreover, helps us to spot the fake alternatives fashioned in fraud, pointing away from God. For instance, to spot a fake dollar bill, it is best to be so familiar with the original that a fake bill will stand out easily. By knowing the Lord profoundly, you can recognize the true God and reject the false gods. And you get a genuine standard to measure yourself against to see how well you match the Original (God). It is a standard higher than yours or anyone else's, worthy of modeling your life after.

God's standard is worth aspiring to because that aspiration frees us from the limitations of lowly thinking. Instead of being earth-bound, we become heaven-bound, free to rise and soar. Soaring with God's help and guidance, we can see the big picture. We can come to understand how the *human bondage to sin and death has held back the human race. True freedom comes from overcoming this bondage* to realize our full potential in God grounded in love (see the chapter "Freedom: Walking in the Way, the Truth and the Life").

Love Wins!

When we love, we counteract the pull of sin which breaks God's law. We hence come to truly reflect the image of God whose essence is love. See 1 Corinthians 13 which gives a detailed exposition of what that love should be in practice as one human relates to another. Walking in love as God commands certainly affects our attitudes and actions. We tend to treat other people better.

As Romans 13:9-10 indicates, God's law consists largely in us loving people, helping them and not harming them. For our benefit, God provides an example in Jesus Christ of how His law through love can be realized and fulfilled in day-to-day human interactions.

By following the loving example and teachings of Jesus, we can come to reflect the fundamental nature of God's love as evidenced in the gospel. When we love as Jesus loves, we defeat sin, making the world a better place and bringing it closer to what God desires.

Key Points in Getting to Know God

Overall, here are some key points to take away here in getting to know God:

(1) *God is love (1 John 4:8) – to love is to know God and God wants us to know Him*

(2) *God loves us deeply which is why Jesus Christ died for our sins (John 3:16)*

(3) *God wants us to love Him (Deuteronomy 10:12)*

(4) *To love God is to love other human beings (1 John 4:20)*

(5) *To love God is to keep His commandments (John 14:23)*

(6) *To obey God is to overcome the sorrows, decay and death that sin brings*

(7) *And with the Holy Spirit guiding us, we get divine help to love everyone, even our enemies.*

God Wants Us to Do Better and to Talk to Him

Because He loves us, God wants us to do better and engage Him. He desires that all the pain, suffering, tears and sorrows in this world ends. He plans to bring them all to an end, defeating sin and death forever. *Sin has so damaged us humans that many do not now look anything like the ultimate image we are supposed to reflect: a loving God.*

In wanting us to do better, God keeps the lines of communications open. He knows we have questions and complaints. The Lord is willing to engage us. So make your case to God today. He is fair and will help you find the answers you seek. Take this now as if God is appealing to you directly through these words in Isaiah 1:18-19 (NKJV):

> "'Come now, and let us reason together,'
> Says the Lord,
> 'Though your sins are like scarlet,
> They shall be as white as snow;
> Though they are red like crimson,
> They shall be as wool.
> If you are willing and obedient,
> You shall eat the good of the land;…'"

Through prayer, you can communicate with God. He wants you to. Make your case to him now directly, *respectfully* in prayer. And stay open for His response and revelations to expand your knowledge.

Don't make the most critical decision in life based on half-knowledge or misinformation. The fate of your soul is too important to ignore. Sincerely seek the truth so that you can make an informed decision. *Get all the facts about God* so that you can make the right choice. The Lord God can help you to *know better* and to *do better in overcoming human limitations* that have doomed so many people.

Victory through Humility

Our biggest limitations can be found in the sin nature and the fallen angels. We need God to overcome them both in this corrupt world – recognizing this stark reality requires humility. *We must acknowledge how weak we are.* We have limited power, limited love and limited self-control. We have limited spiritual insights – we have limited knowledge, period! *We need God's help to make up for our deficiencies.*

Humility helps us to accept God's help and authority over our lives so as to overcome our greatest obstacles! Our humility acknowledge these realities: (1) that we are limited in what we know and understand in the physical and spiritual realms; (2) that our powers are minuscule compared to God's (or the angels); and (3) that we need God desperately.

We need God because we are created in His image – He is the Master, the Original. He was here before us. *We are copies that remain incomplete without the Creator.* To avoid being distorted or diminished, we must be modeled perfectly after the Original. We cannot ignore where we come from and the lessons from the Source, our Maker on how to live. God knows what makes us better, or what makes things worse for us. We cannot know more than He does. We need God!

The Failure of Human Knowledge and Effort

By knowing and deferring to God, we can learn how to survive and thrive for eternity. We can learn how to defeat sin and survive the second death, the ultimate penalty for sin. We can indeed learn how to have the abundant life that Jesus Christ offers (see John 10:10). That abundant life differs markedly from the current and historical state of mankind. It's a perpetual state of siege today with malice, misery, wars, sorrows, diseases, pain, suffering and death everywhere.

Sadly, human knowledge outside of God has failed woefully to solve all of these problems. Imagine how much better the world would be if all of us – without exception – would follow *all* the commandments of God in Deuteronomy 5 in the Holy Bible. Indeed, consider how much life would be better if we all lived perfectly by the greatest commandments as taught by Jesus Christ: to love God and love people (see Mark 12:28-34).

But an alarming number of humans have shown a marked inability to live according to the greatest commandments. That is why we need God's Holy Spirit to enable us have the capacity to love, the power to overcome all evil forces and the self-control to stop from sinning. When we sincerely seek to know God, we will find Him along with solutions to all of our problems – praise God!

Revelations about God in the Bible

For those sincerely seeking the truth, *God gives deep insights about Himself through* the lessons, stories, facts, principles, prophesies and revelations in *the Holy Bible.* The Bible illustrates through the lives of many people how to correctly relate to God, and how wrong choices are at the source of mankind's problems.

The essence of the insights we get from the Bible is that *we must come to God to solve human problems.* Otherwise, human failure is certain. And to get to God, we much go through His Son, Jesus Christ who proclaimed: "I am the way, the truth, and the life: no man cometh unto the Father, but by me" (John 14:6, KJV). Jesus represents the truth about God and the way to get to God for eternal life.

In addition, as John the Baptist testified: "For He whom God has sent speaks the words of God; for He gives the Spirit without measure. The Father loves the Son and has given all things into His hand. He who believes in the Son has eternal life; but he *who does not obey the Son will not see life, but the wrath of God abides on him*" (John 3:34-36, NASB, emphasis added; see also John 1).

The Door to Salvation: Jesus Christ

Jesus is the way to salvation, the door to eternal life: "I am the door; if anyone enters through Me, he will be saved, and will go in and out and find pasture" (John 10:9, NASB). His sacrifice grants access to God for eternal life. "For through Him we both have *access by one Spirit to the Father*" (Ephesians 2:18, NKJV, bold emphasis added). We need Jesus Christ, working through the Holy Spirit, for access to the Heavenly Father God.

In the Son of God, with access to God's vast overcoming power, we undoubtedly find the permanent cure for humanity's problems. In Jesus, we find redemption from the law of sin and death (see the chapter "Freedom: Walking in the Way, the Truth and the Life"). Only the sacrifice by Jesus Christ pays the penalty for sin (while enabling our access to eternal life by God's grace). *Without Jesus, you would have to pay for sin yourself – with your own life.*

With the atonement for sin by Jesus Christ, we have hope. With Jesus, there is resurrection for the dead, and access for believers to dwell in the presence of God forever. The Son is the link to the Heavenly Father. "For *there is* one God and one Mediator between God and men, *the* Man Christ Jesus" (1 Timothy 2:5, NKJV).

As mediator, Jesus brings peace between God and humans (Romans 5:1). He reconciles us to God. He helps us to understand how love wins over sin. As our atonement for sin, *He shows us love by hanging on the cross for our sake*, our substitution in taking the penalty for sin. And He teaches us that to truly love, we must love each other sacrificially (John 15:12-17). *Jesus demonstrates the essence of God in love – praise God!*

Mirror: Jesus Reflects God as We Should

For those sincerely seeking the truth, here is one significant fact about God: Jesus reflects God! We tend to reflect God more, when we are more like Jesus Christ: loving the way He loves and obeying God like He does. To know God truly, to be like God essentially, we need to *learn from and follow the perfect example of Jesus Christ, the Son of God*.

In a conversation long ago, one of His disciples asked Jesus to show them God the Father. "Have I been with you so long, and yet you have not known Me, Philip? He who has seen Me has seen the Father," Jesus responded, continuing: "so how can you say, 'Show us the Father'? Do you not believe that *I am in the Father, and the Father in Me?* The words that I speak to you I do not speak on My own authority; but *the Father who dwells in Me does the works*" (John 14:9-10, NKJV, emphasis added).

Jesus Christ indeed represents and reflects God. *He is God* (John 1). As Paul wrote in Colossians 1:14-20 (KJV), speaking of Jesus:

> "In whom we have redemption through his blood, even the forgiveness of sins:

> Who is the image of the invisible God, the firstborn of every creature:

> For by him were all things created, that are in heaven, and that are in earth, visible and invisible, whether they be thrones, or dominions, or principalities, or powers: all things were created by him, and for him:

And he is before all things, and by him all things consist.

And he is the head of the body, the church: who is the beginning, the firstborn from the dead; that in all things he might have the preeminence.

For it pleased the Father that in him should all fulness dwell;

And, having made peace through the blood of his cross, by him to reconcile all things unto himself; by him, I say, whether they be things in earth, or things in heaven."

A God of Justice, Mercy and Grace

By dying on the cross: (1) Jesus Christ has paid the penalty for sin, so those identified with God can live forever in love, prosperity, peace and joy; (2) Jesus has defeated death by resurrecting from the dead, paving the way for other children of God to do the same in future; (3) Jesus has reconciled believers to God for us to be born again; (4) Jesus has enabled us to be filled with the Holy Spirit so we can forever overcome the corruption of sin and walk in God's true image of love; (5) Jesus enables us to rise up to our full potential in God, helping us to *know better and do better;* (6) by God's grace through His Son, we can therefore escape the wrath of God against sin; and (7) believers get to inherit all the numerous benefits of being citizens of heaven. Praise God!

Thankfully, Jesus has paid the penalty for our sins. So we don't have to pay that debt. If however we reject God's salvation plan, we stand exposed to judgment: eternal condemnation. A holy God of justice cannot be expected to overlook forever the corruption of life that comes from sin or the devil and other fallen angels. Sin distorts God's image in us, corrupting life.

A corrupted life is a diminished life, reducing unsaved humans to a state of inexorable decay that has doomed this world to everlasting destruction. *Although the wrath of God remains on those who reject salvation, His mercy and grace is freely offered to all through Jesus Christ.*

If you haven't already done so, please accept Jesus Christ today. And come to fully realize your potential as one created in God's image. Let the Son of God help you gain a deeper knowledge of God based on love. Say this short prayer now: *Dear God, please help me — save me! I want to know You. I confess my sins, and acknowledge that Jesus Christ, my Lord and Savior, died for me and rose from the dead to give me eternal life. I need You, Lord! Help me please to reflect Your image and become a vessel of Your love to others through the Holy Spirit. In Jesus name I pray, Amen!*

Discussion Questions

---

1. Who is God – why should you know Him? What should you get to know about the Creator of the universe?

2. What is God's relationship with humans and why does our Maker love us so much?

3. How can you get to know God and embrace the divine love and salvation offered through Jesus Christ?

Chapter 17

Spiritual Intelligence

Spiritual Intelligence: Of Sights and Insights

Highlights:

- There is more to life than meets the eye, more to know or see than the human eye or general senses can naturally perceive.
- We are not alone: there is God, Jesus Christ, the Holy Spirit and many, many angels (holy or wicked).
- God gives spiritual sights and insights to those who believe in Him, enabling access to information far beyond normal human perceptions.

The king was puzzled and troubled. How could his war plans keep ending up in the ears of his enemy? Calling his servants, he asked: "Will you tell me which of us is for the king of Israel?" One of them replied: "No, my lord, O king; but Elisha, the prophet who is in Israel, tells the king of Israel the words that you speak in your bedroom." The king ordered: "Go and see where he is, that I may send and take him" (2 Kings 6:11-13, NASB).

After pinpointing Elisha's location, the king sent "horses, and chariots, and a great host: and they came by night, and compassed the city about" (2 Kings 6:14, KJV). What the king of Syria did not realize was the power of spiritual intelligence which is available to believers in God. Like many others who think they can plot in secret to harm God's servants, he could have saved himself a lot of trouble. But he was spiritually obtuse.

The king's military response ignored one simple fact. God could reveal a plot against the king of Israel to the Prophet Elisha, correct? If so, wouldn't God also expose a plot against his very own prophet? Check out what happened next when Elisha's servant went out early in the morning. The servant saw "an army, surrounding the city with horses and chariots," and asked: "Alas, my master! What shall we do?" (2 Kings 6:15, NKJV).

The servant had eyes to see things in the natural realm, but lacked the ultimate in vision: spiritual sight and insight. "Fear not," Elisha answered: "for they that be with us are more than they that be with them." And the prophet requested, "Lord, I pray thee, open his eyes, that he may see". When the Lord opened his eyes, the servant saw that "the mountain was full of horses and chariots of fire round about Elisha" (2 Kings 6:16-17, KJV). Wow – praise God!

You should read the rest of the story from 2 Kings 6:18 onward. Similarly, there are other stories in the Holy Bible detailing how God often offers uncommon information, deep insights to believers. In ancient Egypt, for instance, God gave Joseph the interpretation to Pharaoh's dreams (Genesis 41). In another instance, "the heavens were opened" and the Prophet Ezekiel "saw visions of God" (Ezekiel 1:1, ESV). Read more about what God revealed to the prophet in the book of Ezekiel.

Furthermore, in yet another instance, God revealed to Daniel what King Nebuchadnezzar *had dreamt of* and *its interpretation!* To test his 'wise men' the king had refused to reveal his dream, insisting that they tell him *both* the dream and its interpretation. They could not. But Daniel and his friends prayed to God, and the Lord answered.

Daniel told the king: "No wise men, enchanters, magicians, or astrologers can show to the king the mystery that the king has asked, but *there is a God in heaven who reveals mysteries,* and he has made known to King Nebuchadnezzar what will be in the latter days. Your dream and the visions of your head as you lay in bed are these…" (Daniel 2:27-28, ESV, emphasis added).

Be sure to prayerfully study the insights that God gave to Daniel and compare them to the book of Revelation. From my personal experience, I know it is very important to always pray for the Holy Spirit to help us gain the insights we need as we study to understand the mysteries of God. "Now we have received not the spirit of the world, but *the Spirit who is from God, that we might understand* the things freely given us by God" (1 Corinthians 2:12, ESV, emphasis added).

All-seeing and all-knowing, God provides revelations, visions and intelligence. He gives specific insights available only to those He calls His own, those who make the things of God their priority in life. And you are His own when you get saved (see the chapter "Salvation: Life in Abundance Forever").

As a child of God, your access to spiritual intelligence from the Lord opens you up to a whole new world of revelations. God gives you deep insights into the mysteries of life. As aided by the Holy Spirit, you come to grasp Biblical teachings on the mysteries of God beyond your own capabilities (see 1 Corinthians 2:11-16).

With the Spirit of truth as your guide, you can gain profound knowledge about God, life, angels and people. Your understanding helps you to thrive in a world where most people are clueless about what is *really* going on in life. On the whole, you come to appreciate more the value of God's love leading you to eternal life.

Fundamentally, you have an edge if saved (a believer in God). Spiritual intelligence gives you a divine advantage for life. You are a child of God, yes, a joint heir with Jesus Christ. So God looks out for you. And by God's grace with the Holy Spirit working in you, you get access to information possible only with God.

On the whole, your victory is assured over everybody and everything that comes against you. Through God's power, you are able to prevail against human and spiritual forces of wickedness. You win because God helps you to rise above your limited human position, power and perception.

All praises to the Most High God! The Lord reigns forever and grants spiritual sights, insights and might to His beloved children! Thank You Lord! We are forever grateful, Heavenly Father! You are most merciful, gracious and loving! We love you, Lord God! Thank You!

Discussion Questions

---

1. What is spiritual intelligence from God – as depicted in the experiences of Elisha, Daniel, Joseph, Ezekiel and John?

2. How can we obtain deep spiritual insights about life and the things of God? From reading 1 Corinthians 2:10-12 (and the whole chapter), what is the role of the Holy Spirit here?

3. Can the enemies of God also provide information – why should they not be trusted and how can you know the difference?

Chapter 18

Freedom

Freedom: Walking in the Way, the Truth and the Life

Highlights:

*   Out of love, God offers us freedom from slavery to the law of sin and death.
*   Those freed are saved to enjoy the abundant life and avoid the fate of all who reject God.
*   True freedom comes from:
    (1) walking under the direction of the Holy Spirit to stay on the right **pathway** to becoming fruitful forever,
    (2) knowing the **truth** about life and death through the redeeming work of Jesus Christ, and
    (3) gaining the soul for **eternal life** by God's grace from the clutches of sin and death.

Freed from the law of sin and death, believers can attain their full potentials as children of God. We can "mount up with wings as eagles" (Isaiah 40:31, KJV), soaring to heights of achievements that can only come through the power of God. Instead of chains we get crowns, replacing condemnation with salvation! Praise God!

"There is therefore now no condemnation to those who are in Christ Jesus, who do not walk according to the flesh, but according to the Spirit. *For the law of the Spirit of life in Christ Jesus has made me free from the law of sin and death*" (Romans 8:1-2*, NKJV, emphasis added). Just like an eagle or an aircraft can soar, defying the law of gravity, so can believers *by God's grace* rise above the law of sin and death. Through the Holy Spirit, we can come under another law. By complying with "the law of the Spirit of life" believers become free in Christ Jesus, gaining the abundant life forever – praise God!

True freedom indeed comes from God through Jesus Christ setting us free from slavery to sin and death. "For what the Law could not do, weak as it was through the flesh, God *did*: sending His own Son in the likeness of sinful flesh and *as an offering* for sin, He condemned sin in the flesh, so that **the requirement of the Law might be fulfilled in us, who do not walk according to the flesh but according to the Spirit**" (Romans 8:3-4, NASB, bold emphasis added). The Son of God demonstrated conclusively with the Spirit how to fulfill God's law – praise God!

Victory over Obstacles to Eternal Life

Without the option God offers through Jesus Christ, all humans throughout the ages would be doomed. We would be condemned to enslavement by sin and death. But through the Holy Spirit dwelling in believers, we become free, gaining the ultimate in power, love and self-control. We become victorious, ultimately overcoming sin and death forever – and only by God's grace!

Historically, because of bondage to sin, death is a debt all humans owe and must pay. For those not saved, this debt terminates the path to eternal life and God's tremendous benefits. Two ways exist to handle this grave debt:

1. You can pay it yourself ("the law of sin and death") – this option means you give up eternal life, separated from God forever: you are not saved.
2. Or Jesus Christ pays it for you ("the law of the Spirit of life") – in this option, you get eternal life: you're born again by the Spirit into the kingdom of heaven, ultimately living with God forever: you are saved.

Please choose wisely. In Jesus Christ, we find the right choice and the truth about life, eternal life. It is *only through the Son of God that death,* the ultimate consequence of mankind's rebellion against God, *is dealt with conclusively* (see Genesis 3 and Romans 1-16). The option offered through Jesus Christ provides victory essentially over two primary obstacles to human progress in a diseased world: (a) our sinful nature, and (b) the spiritual forces of evil. Over the ages, human efforts have failed woefully to defeat or overcome these obstacles.

But God provides freedom from them all. Believers get help from the Holy Spirit to overcome the sinful nature, while the power of God shields us from "the spiritual *forces* of wickedness in the heavenly *places*" (Ephesians 6:12, NASB). Eventually, when this world ends, believers survive into eternity, freed from all the human problems we see today (see Revelation 21, 1 Thessalonians 4:16-19, Revelation 20:6, John 11:25 and 1 Corinthians 15:22-24).

Maintaining Our Freedom

To ensure that we don't fail, the freedom that we get from God needs to be maintained. "It was for freedom that Christ set us free; therefore keep standing firm and do not be subject again to a yoke of slavery" (Galatians 5:1, NASB). After throwing off the shackles of slavery to sin and death, it would be foolhardy for us to go back into bondage.

Our sinful nature (and the fallen angels, as well as other sinful humans) will keep trying to pull us back, away from God. To prevail as winners and over-comers, we must come and stay under the direction of the Holy Spirit. There is no room for diversions, deviations or distractions.

"For if you live by its dictates, you will die. But if *through the power of the Spirit you put to death the deeds of your sinful nature*, you will live" (Romans 8:13, NLT, emphasis added; see also Galatians 5:13-26). The Spirit helps believers to resist the sinful nature. We therefore can stay anchored in God's way, eternally secured under the most powerful force in the universe. By crying out frequently and watchfully in prayer, *helped by the Holy Spirit* (see Romans 8:26), we can resist the temptation to sin (see Matthew 26:41).

The Way to God for Eternal Life

Helping us to stay the course in God's way of love, the work of the Holy Spirit is invaluable to believers. Assuredly, as Jesus promised: "I will ask the Father, and He will give you another Helper, that He may be with you forever"

(John 14:16, NASB – see also the chapter: "The Holy Spirit: Power, Love and Self-Control"). The Spirit indeed keeps believers anchored in God, helping us to stay steadfast and free on the road to eternity in the kingdom of heaven.

At the end of the road, eventually, *we will all stand before God* for judgement – see Revelation 20:12-15 (KJV):

> "And I saw the dead, small and great, stand before God; and the books were opened: and another book was opened, which is the book of life: and the dead were judged out of those things which were written in the books, according to their works.
>
> And the sea gave up the dead which were in it; and death and hell delivered up the dead which were in them: and they were judged every man according to their works.
>
> And death and hell were cast into the lake of fire. This is the second death.
>
> And whosoever was not found written in the book of life was cast into the lake of fire."

By God's grace, death is vanquished for believers – praise the Lord! We get to be with the Lord for eternity – praise God! Sadly, nonbelievers will be cast into the lake of fire. It doesn't have to be so. God has provided salvation for all through Jesus Christ. Indeed, it is only through the redemptive work of Jesus Christ that we can be set free from sin and its ultimate consequence: the second death.

Significantly, it is only through Jesus that we can get access to God for eternal life. As Jesus Himself noted: "I am *the way, and the truth, and the life*; no one comes to the Father *but through Me*" (John 14:6, NASB, emphasis added: see also Ephesians 2:18 and John 3:3-6).

Furthermore, "If we receive the witness of men, the witness of God is greater; for this is the witness of God which He has testified of His Son. He who believes in the Son of God has the witness in himself; he who does not believe God has made Him a liar, because he has not believed the testimony that God has given of His Son. And this is the testimony: that *God has given us eternal life, and this life is in His Son. He who has the Son has life; he who does not have the Son of God does not have life*" wrote the apostle John, (1 John 5:9-12, NKJV, emphasis added).

The Truth about Life and Death

In Jesus Christ, essentially, we find *the truth* about *life* and death. We find *the way* for the soul to gain eternal life and be with God forever. In Jesus Christ, we discover the way to enjoy the endless benefits available only to believers in God. There is everlasting freedom, peace, love, joy, fulfillment, prosperity, success, pleasures and more for those who love God. Sin unfortunately has shortchanged mankind's access to these great benefits in God. Thankfully, our reconciliation with God through the atonement for sin by Jesus Christ opens the door to these benefits.

Prophesies about Jesus the Messiah

Historically, multiple prophesies foretold the coming of the Messiah, Jesus Christ (see Romans 1:2-3 and Isaiah 53). And when the Son of God came, He proclaimed the kingdom of heaven, atoning for our sins and opening our access to eternal life. Jesus Christ opened the way for us all to: (a) obtain forgiveness for sin, (b) gain eternal life and (c) enjoy the tremendous benefits available only to the children of God. And not everyone is a child of God – you have to be saved to become one.

Demonstrating God's compassion and power throughout time, Jesus Christ provides freedom even for those who died before His crucifixion and resurrection (see Romans 2:1-16, John 5:24-30, Romans 4:3 and Jeremiah 17:9-10). Those who *walked in God's way* like Abraham, Isaac, Jacob, Joseph, Moses, Elijah, David, Daniel and others are covered. And as Daniel was told: "But as for you, go *your way* to the end; then you will enter into rest and rise *again* for your allotted portion at the end of the age" (Daniel 12:13, NASB). *They all*, like believers in God today, *are redeemed from the law of sin and death through the atonement for sin by Jesus Christ.* Praise God!

Love: the Solution to Human Problems

For a very long time, unfortunately, the law of sin and death has held the human race hostage to a tortured existence. The consequences of sin have been manifested in the vicious circle of human problems: conflicts, wars, crimes, hunger, diseases, destitutions and deaths (please review Deuteronomy 5, Deuteronomy 28 and Romans 5-8).

Surely, as history has shown, human problems are not solvable by human hands. Only the hand of God steering humans can. Amazingly, the solution to our problems is within reach. Enabled by the Holy Spirit, we can follow God's commandment to, essentially: *(1) love God,* and *(2) love our neighbors.* It's not complicated!

God-inspired and centered love entails that we do no wrong or harm to other humans. "For this, 'YOU SHALL NOT COMMIT ADULTERY, YOU SHALL NOT MURDER, YOU SHALL NOT STEAL, YOU SHALL NOT COVET,' and if there is any other commandment, it is summed up in this saying, 'YOU SHALL LOVE YOUR NEIGHBOR AS YOURSELF.' Love does no wrong to a neighbor; therefore love is the fulfillment of *the* law" (Romans 13:9-10, NASB; see also Matthew 22:36-40).

Basically, if you cannot obey all of the commands above faultlessly, underscored by a genuinely loving and giving attitude, *then you are in bondage to sin and death.* You need redemption because you are a danger to fellow humans and to yourself.

Why Do Humans Have Laws?

Indeed, *God's commandments are for human benefit* – all humans. Consider this critical question: why do all societies have laws, rules or regulations? It is because *there is something about the human nature (the sinful nature) that requires restraining or regulation* (to curtail lawlessness or anarchy).

Distinctly, the Bible paints a disturbing picture regarding the state of the human heart: "The heart is deceitful above all things, and desperately wicked: who can know it? I the Lord search the heart, I try the reins, even to give every man according to his ways, and according to the fruit of his doings" (Jeremiah 17:9-10, KJV). Of course, the desperately wicked human heart is prone to doing desperately wicked deeds.

So, if we can agree that human conduct (our default behavior: wickedness) requires regulation, then the question remains: *which rules, laws or regulations are best for humans?* Would it not make better sense to go with the laws or commandments God? After all, God is the Creator of humankind. Who else understands better our very essence? *God designed us and knows what is best for us in solving human problems while preserving our life and liberty for eternity* (see Genesis 1:26-27, Deuteronomy 5, Romans 13:9-14, John 1-3 and Romans 8).

Indeed, obeying God's commandments – walking in His way grounded in love – offers the greatest freedom. To maintain our walk, to persevere in God's way, we need to stay under the direction of the Holy Spirit. And *when the fruit of the Spirit is fully realized, human freedom reigns supreme, unrestrained*: "But the fruit of the Spirit is love, joy, peace, patience, kindness, goodness, faithfulness, gentleness, self-control; *against such things there is no law*" (Galatians 5:23-24, NASB, emphasis added).

What Freedom Do You Really Have?

Realistically, what freedom do you actually have when you are constantly weighed down by human problems and could end up losing your soul forever? Are you truly free from bondage to sin and death? *Aided by the Holy Spirit*, our true freedom comes from aligning our mindsets and actions with the commandments of God as illustrated by Jesus Christ. Our true freedom, basically, comes from walking in God's way as enabled by Jesus Christ working through the Holy Spirit.

Genuine freedom comes from the Son of God destroying the shackles of sin and death in our lives. And as Jesus noted: "Truly, truly, I say to you, ***everyone who practices sin is a slave to sin***. The slave does not remain in the house forever; the son remains forever. So ***if the Son sets you free, you will be free indeed***" (John 8:34-36, ESV, bold emphasis added).

Overcoming the Dark Side

Freed by the Son of God, believers get to inherit all the benefits of God's kingdom – praise the Lord! In fact, the kingdom of heaven remains the best option to solve human problems. The truth is that, we have had enough experience experimenting with human ideas, ideologies, lifestyles and practices, yet human problems persist. Hatred persists. Hunger persists. Misery persists. Mass murders persist. Greed persists. Crimes persist. Wars persist. Sorrows persist.

There is definitely something about the dark side of human nature that defies human solutions. Only the way of God works. *Love works.* Freedom in God works. *Walking in the Spirit of God works.* Thankfully, we have hope in God. The Lord is able to free us from slavery to sin and death, if we let Him. Praise God that we can be enabled, empowered by the Holy Spirit to fulfill His law!

Anchored in the Spirit of Truth

Speaking of God, a psalmist wrote: "Your righteousness is an everlasting righteousness. And Your law is truth" (Psalm 119:142, NKJV). Certainly, the right way to live is by God's law: everything else is a lie. And surely, as noted by Paul, we do have "in the Law the embodiment of knowledge and of the truth" (Romans 2:20, NASB).

Undoubtedly, there is freedom in knowledge, in knowing the truth. "Then Jesus said to those Jews who believed Him, 'If you abide in My word, you are My disciples indeed. And you shall *know the truth, and the truth shall make you free*" (John 8:31-32, NKJV, emphasis added).

Moreover, as the apostle John wrote: "And we know that the Son of God has come, and has given us understanding so that we may know Him who is true; and *we are in Him who is true, in His Son Jesus Christ*. This is the *true God and eternal life*" (1 John 5:20, NASB, emphasis added).

To stay anchored in the truth, in Jesus Christ, believers can rely on the Holy Spirit, known as "the Spirit of truth" (John 14:17, KJV). We therefore can avoid spiritual ignorance which is dangerous. Ignorance darkens our paths, hiding the truth about life from our sights. It makes us vulnerable to lies, especially from the devil described by Jesus as "the father of lies" (John 8:44, NASB).

Victims of Devilish Deceptions

Many unfortunately have fallen victim to devilish deceptions: "in whose case the god of this world has blinded the minds of the unbelieving so that they might not see the light of the gospel of the glory of Christ, who is the image of God" (2 Corinthians 4:4, NASB). Compounding and confusing matters for those not being led by the Holy Spirit, the devil can even pretend to be an angel of light (see 2 Corinthians 11:14-15).

Sadly, these victims of ignorance and deceptions are condemned to a circumscribed and doomed existence (see Isaiah 5:13 and Hosea 4:6). They have limited knowledge. They come to life, withering away and then die, souls lost forever. It doesn't have to be that way.

By God's grace, we can all – by getting saved – have access to the deep understanding, the hidden treasures, and the tremendous benefits available only to believers. Salvation comes to those who draw near, or cry out to God for help, those who give up wickedness and embrace love. *Why don't you call out to God now, if you are not saved?*

Empowered for Greatness

Mercifully, those saved avoid the perils of rejecting God. Graciously, the Lord empowers believers to do exceedingly great things through Jesus Christ, our Lord and Savior. Moreover, believers get the inside view, the enhanced insights into the mysteries of life and the matchless blessings reserved for those who love God.

"But as it is written: 'Eye has not seen, nor ear heard, nor have entered into the heart of man the things which God has prepared for those who love Him.' But God has revealed them to us through His Spirit. For the Spirit searches all things, yes, the deep things of God," wrote the apostle Paul (1 Corinthians 2:9-10, NKJV).

If you are a nonbeliever, you are denied access to the spiritual insights God gives to believers (see the chapter "*Spiritual Intelligence: Of Sights and Insights*"). With God enabling us spiritually, believers can discern the things of God, becoming empowered and enlightened to walk in His way (see 1 Corinthians 2:12-14 and Romans 8:5-39).

To aid us in God's way, Jesus offered the Divine Helper: "When the Helper comes, whom I will send to you from the Father, *that is* the Spirit of truth who proceeds from the Father, He will testify about Me" (John 15:26, NASB; see also John 20:22 and Acts 2:4).

The Holy Spirit, the Spirit of truth, keeps us anchored in the truth – in Jesus Christ, the Word of God – so we can be fruitful. "I am the vine, you *are* the branches. He who abides in Me, and I in him, bears much fruit; for without

Me you can do nothing" (John 15:5, NKJV; see also Galatians 5:22-26). By staying connected to Jesus Christ through the Spirit, we are empowered for greatness, walking in God's way, resisting sin and yielding much good fruit. Praise God!

Sin, Anarchy and Lawlessness

But for those not walking in the Spirit, sin is their master. Bearing bad fruit (Galatians 5:19-21), they can do great harm. They do not respect God's law grounded in love. "Everyone who practices sin also practices lawlessness; and **sin is lawlessness**," so noted the apostle John (1 John 3:4, NASB, bold emphasis added). Anarchy is largely not popular in societies. Legal restraints are therefore needed. And concerning which laws work best, to repeat a point made earlier, *there is none better than God's commandments, proven to make humans better.*

"But we know that the Law is good, if one uses it lawfully, realizing the fact that law is not made for a righteous person, but for those who are lawless and rebellious, for the ungodly and sinners, for the unholy and profane, for those who kill their fathers or mothers, for murderers and immoral men and homosexuals and kidnappers and liars and perjurers, and whatever else is contrary to sound teaching" (1 Timothy 1:8-10, NASB).

The Spirit of Life in Christ Jesus

Thanks be to God because "the Spirit of life in Christ Jesus" empowers us to stay free from sin and defeat death. The Spirit helps us to counteract, yes, conquer the proclivity that contorts human hearts into being so "desperately wicked". We instead become full of good works – praise God! Yes, we stand redeemed. Believers are debt-free from death. Christ has set us free! We don't have to pay the debt for sin – praise God!

By manifesting the fruit of the Spirit, believers demonstrate the power of God to free us all from the law of sin and death. *Under the Spirit of truth, we get to walk in true freedom.* We get to walk in the way, the truth and the life – Jesus Christ! "For the Lord is the Spirit, and wherever the Spirit of the Lord is, there is freedom" (2 Corinthians 3:17, NLT). Praise God!

Important Notice

If you are still in bondage to the law of sin and death, let God help you now though Jesus Christ. Say this prayer now: *Dear God, please rescue me from the law of sin and death. I acknowledge I am a sinner – please forgive me. Help me! I accept Jesus Christ as my Lord and Savior, and acknowledge that He died for my sins and was raised by the Holy Spirit. Please fill me up with the Holy Spirit so that I can be free to do Your will and share Your love with others. In Jesus name I pray, amen! Thank You, Lord!*

Reference

- *Be sure to contact Calvary Chapel Philadelphia for an excellent message titled *"The Law of the Spirit Romans 8:2-9"* delivered by Don McClure on Sunday AM April 26, 2015 (www.ccphilly.org / 215-969-1520).

Discussion Questions

1. What is the law of sin and death and how does it affect humans?

2. What is the law of the Spirit of life in Christ Jesus and how can it set you free from the law of sin and death?

3. Why did Jesus Christ describe Himself as the way, the truth and the life?

Chapter 19

Prosperity

Prosperity: Riches in Jesus Christ, Rich toward God

Highlights:

- The Son of God became poor temporarily so that we could become rich, sacrificing Himself for our salvation into true, everlasting riches.
- With our riches, with our prosperity comes the responsibility to invest in other people, while maintaining an attitude of contentment regardless of our fortunes in this passing world.
- The ultimate prosperity is eternal life for those who put their faith in God. Believers inherit a new world filled with joyous abundance, riches beyond measure, but free from our present troubles and sorrows – praise God!

"For you know the grace of our Lord Jesus Christ, that though He was rich, yet for your sakes He became poor, that you through His poverty might become rich," so wrote the apostle Paul (2 Corinthians 8:9, NKJV; see also John 10:7-12). Through Jesus Christ, God has opened the door to eternal riches, providing everlasting prosperity: life in abundance forever. You must be saved, however, to pass through that door.

Indeed, from the perspective of the following prayer by the apostle John, the riches – the prosperity – that God offers is multifaceted: "Beloved, I pray that you may prosper in all things and be in health, *just as your soul prospers*" (3 John 1:2, NKJV, emphasis added). We are spirit, soul *and* body (see 1 Thessalonians 5:23). Therefore, our focus should not be only on the body. Our prosperity must be complete, encompassing all that we are made of: *spirit, soul* and *body.*

Great Wealth: Abraham and Solomon

Like the Patriarch Abraham or King Solomon, believers in God can have great wealth in this world, even becoming billionaires or greater. While that may be quite wonderful, God has much more in store for us. *There's much more to life than wealth in this world which is passing away.* Believers get to inherit a new world with immeasurable riches in Christ Jesus – praise God!

In the age to come, believers also get incorruptible bodies: free of pain, disease and death (see Philippians 3:20-21 and 1 Corinthians 15:42). *There's not enough gold in this world to buy all that.* Absolutely no amount of money can buy your salvation, or make you a child of God and a partaker of the divine nature with a new, perfect body.

Note please that this is not to belittle the great wealth believers can still have in this world (or diminish the good it can be used for). It can be quite substantial. Certainly, *our benefits in God are both in this world and in the one to come,* but the new world holds much more because it is everlasting.

In an illuminating exchange with Jesus Christ, the apostle Peter remarked: "See, we have left all and followed You". To which, Jesus responded: "Assuredly, I say to you, there is no one who has left house or parents or brothers or wife or children, for the sake of the kingdom of God, who shall not *receive many times more in this present time, and in the age to come eternal life*" (Luke 18:28-30, NKJV, emphasis added). Believers can have great wealth now, and expect much more definitely in the coming new age for eternity – praise God!

The Full Measure of our Prosperity in God

It is in the age to come that it will be revealed the full measure of our prosperity in God. This world as we know it is marked for destruction "in which the heavens will pass away with a roar and the elements will be destroyed with intense heat, and the earth and its works will be burned up" (2 Peter 3:10,

NASB). "Nevertheless we, according to His promise, look for new heavens and a new earth in which righteousness dwells" (2 Peter 3:13, NKJV – see also the last chapter of this book: "New World: No More Sorrow").

Pending the revelation of the new world, believers can invest time, treasures and talents in promoting the kingdom of God *by loving people*. Eventually, as joint-heirs with the resurrected Christ, believers in God get *everything*. We inherit all the goodness and abundance of God's kingdom, in all its limitless riches and glory. We get to experience the ultimate prosperity of the soul: eternal life in *abundance in God's presence forever* – praise the Lord!

So don't be deceived. There are serious limitations to how far riches in this world can take you. *Wealth or prosperity without the soul secured for eternity is worthless ultimately*. Why? Consider this critical question from Jesus Christ in Mark 8:36 (KJV): "For what shall it profit a man, if he shall gain the whole world, and lose his own soul?" Beware that there is a coming judgment for all peoples. Only those saved will survive and thrive. Others lose their souls. The world as we know it will pass away. Only what is invested in the kingdom of heaven will last.

Investing in People, Investing in Heaven

By helping people, loving them as God directs us to do, we are investing in the kingdom of heaven. It means we are showing our love for our Heavenly Father by loving people. For to love God is to love people. Both cannot be separated. The key is to invest in heaven by investing in people.

"Do not store up for yourselves treasures on earth, where moth and rust destroy, and where thieves break in and steal," Jesus declared. "But store up for yourselves treasures in heaven, where neither moth nor rust destroys, and where thieves do not break in or steal; for where your treasure is, there your heart will be also" (Matthew 6:19-21, NASB).

On how to store treasures in heaven, Jesus provided clear directions. "If you want to be perfect, go, sell what you have and give to the poor, and you will have treasure in heaven; and come follow Me," Jesus told a wealthy man who had asked what good deed he must do to get eternal life (Matthew 19:21, NKJV; see also Luke 18:18-23). *When we invest in heaven, our wealth is secured forever* – it is not dependent on the vagaries of Wall Street or the global financial markets!

Rich toward God

By investing in heaven, we avoid becoming like the rich man spoken of by Jesus in Luke 12. The man's land yielded so much that he ran out of room to store his crops. So he decided to take down his barns and builder bigger ones. He figured that with so much stored up for himself, he would have enough for many years to take things easy: eating, drinking and merrymaking.

"But God said to him, 'You fool! This *very* night your soul is required of you; and *now* who will own what you have prepared?' So is the man who stores up treasure for himself, and is not rich toward God'" (Luke 12:20-21, NASB). What better way to be rich toward God than to help the less fortunate out of love for God?

Note: God is not against eating, drinking and merrymaking – remember: Jesus Christ turned water into wine at a wedding (John 2). And He fed multitudes miraculously. The point being made here is that we are to love our neighbors as ourselves with our wealth. *Our prosperity (property or possessions) should be shared with others,* **not** *hoarded.*

Our Love for God and People

In obedience to God's commandment to love our neighbors, we all have a responsibility to share our wealth with others. "We know love by this, that He laid down His life for us; and we ought to lay down our lives for the brethren. *But whoever has the world's goods, and sees his brother in need and closes his heart against him, how does the love of God abide in him?* Little children, let us not love with word or with tongue, but in deed and truth," wrote the apostle John (1 John 3:16-18, NASB, emphasis added; see also 1 Timothy 6:17-19 and Luke 18:18-23).

When we help the less privileged among us, our generosity is toward God Himself in whose image, like us, they are created. We are essentially being rich toward God: "Assuredly, I say to you, inasmuch as you did *it* to one of the least of these My brethren, you did *it* to Me" (Matthew 25:40, NKJV; see also Luke 14:12-14).

Significantly, your good deeds are never in vain. Note that **God will reward you for helping the less fortunate**. "But when you give a feast, invite the poor, the crippled, the lame, the blind, and you will be blessed, because they cannot repay you. *For you will be repaid at the resurrection of the just*" (Luke 14:13-14, ESV, emphasis added). Moreover, as Jesus Christ is quoted as saying (and Pastor Jim Cymbala of the Brooklyn Tabernacle emphasizes): "It is more blessed to give than to receive" (Acts 20:35, ESV).

Generosity to help others without expecting anything in return from them demonstrates our selfless love for people and hence for God. Love unquestionably is at the core of God's commandments (Matthew 22:35-41): to love God and love people. A mindset of selfless love emphasizes giving to others, not taking or stealing from them.

On the contrary, a mindset that is focused on taking or stealing from others can quickly become predatory. Fueled by greed (as well as pride and hatred), it lacks contentment, one of the character-building blocks that God desires in us all. A predatory mindset has no qualms about inflicting pain on others to get its way. Remember Romans 13:10 (NKJV): "Love does no harm to a neighbor..."

Greed hurts people. It is not in the way or will of God – indeed *the covetous (or greedy) cannot inherit the kingdom of God* (see Ephesians 5:5). In God's provision for mankind, no one should have to go daily without their basic needs fulfilled. But not enough people are willing to share their wealth. In fact, there are many who would even deny others the basic necessities of life. Is it any surprise then that, *although we have enough food to go around in this world, people still starve?* Why is that?

Admittedly, there are many generous people around – unfortunately, they are not enough.

Provisions for God's Children

Even in a world of desperate want, anyway, God still provides for His children (believers). Even in dire times, as the stories of Jacob, Joseph and others illustrate, God makes a way for believers. The Lord God knows what we need and has proven over the ages to be quite faithful in fulfilling our needs – praise God! Graciously, *the Lord provides us with the wisdom, the ability, the resources and the diligence to generate wealth.* We just need to seek His guidance to ensure that our prosperity is forever.

Even in a corrupt world where greed and perversion have distorted God's provision for people's needs, the Creator still provides. The Lord makes a way for His children to be fulfilled. And out of the abundance of bounteous blessings from God, believers are then able to give to others (see 2 Corinthians 9:8). In doing so, we help alleviate the sufferings of many.

For believers, moreover, God works in different ways through the conditions in our various phases of life to test and shape our characters. As part of a divine character-building plan, God works through what He allows our way, or holds back from us for our good. God may initially trust us with a certain measure of wealth or talent to see how well we can handle it. If we conduct ourselves properly, God is more likely to trust us with much more (see Luke 16:10, Matthew 25:14-30 and 2 Corinthians 9:6-8).

Character-Building: an Attitude of Contentment

While faithfully handling whatever we may be blessed with in a particular phase of life, believers have an opportunity to embrace Godly character-building. We can learn to develop an attitude of contentment spoken of by the apostle Paul.

"Not that I speak from want, for I have learned to be content in whatever circumstances I am," Paul wrote. "*I know how to get along with humble means, and I also know how to live in prosperity*; in any and every circumstance I have learned the secret of being filled and going hungry, both of having abundance and suffering need. *I can do all things through Him who strengthens me*" (Philippians 4:11-13, NASB, emphasis added).

Our faith in God, certainly, reinforces our attitude of contentment. Through the Holy Spirit, believers can trust in God's presence to strengthen and sustain us through all conditions. There is no reason for despair. And we don't need to be dependent on any other source but on God. "Keep your life free from love of money, and be content with what you have, for he has said, '*I will never leave you nor forsake you*'" (Hebrews 13:5, ESV, bold emphasis added).

With help from the Holy Spirit, believers can resist the temptation to replace God with material things as the object of our worship or love. *Faith consists in believing what God says*. Be assured of this: God will never abandon the believer. As the psalmist wrote: "I have been young and now I am old, Yet I have not seen the righteous forsaken Or his descendants begging bread" (Psalm 37:25, NASB).

God who owns all the riches in the universe *does not and cannot forsake His own children*. He feeds the birds of the air and provides for the enormous appetites of the giant whales. He certainly can, and *will always provide for the believer* – it is an assurance that promotes a mindset of contentment. That mindset can help guard against a dangerous attachment to money or material possessions.

Putting God First vs. the Love of Money

Let's be clear: there is nothing wrong with money in of itself. *Indeed, great wealth can be used for great good.* It is the *love of money* that is dangerous. "For ***the love of money*** is a root of all *kinds of* evil, for which some have strayed from the faith in their greediness, and pierced themselves through with many sorrows. But you, O man of God, flee these things and pursue righteousness, godliness, faith, love, patience, gentleness" (1 Timothy 6:10-11, NKJV, bold emphasis added).

Admittedly, believers may at different times be challenged to make do with less. Such challenges may increase the temptation to depend on money, or to become obsessed with it or to degenerate into greediness. Countering that temptation requires a deep trust in God. It entails believing that the Lord will provide for all of our needs, regardless of the situation. *Believers don't have to cut corners and commit sin to be fulfilled.* And as the apostle Paul noted: "And my God will supply all your needs according to His riches in glory in Christ Jesus" (Philippians 4:19, NASB; see also Romans 8:32).

Even as millionaires, billionaires or better, believers cannot be distracted from a focus on God in faith. The Lord needs to be the focus of our love, service and worship, not money or wealth. After all, Abraham was rich but he still put God first to the point of obeying God to give up his only son (see Genesis 22)! And as Jesus noted: "No one can serve two masters; for either he will hate the one and love the other, or he will be devoted to one and despise the other. You cannot serve God and wealth" (Matthew 6:24, NASB). Significantly, because *God is the ultimate source and owner of all wealth, the love of money over God is quite out of order.*

Indeed, the love of money is a love not of God and hence not of people: for to love God is to love people. The love of money may so twist a person's heart that money could become the god to be worshipped and loved. Such a twisted love can promote dependence on material things for fulfillment. It ignores the true God who is the ultimate creator of wealth and the source of enduring success and satisfaction. Such a twisted love goes hand-in-hand with greed which can never satisfy (see the chapter: "Satisfaction beyond Measure").

Lessons from the Global Financial Crash

Moreover, as Jesus cautioned: "Take heed and beware of covetousness, for one's life does not consist in the abundance of the things he possesses" (Luke 12:15, NKJV). There is definitely more to life than material possessions. Such possessions are not even reliable. So why trust in them? The global financial crash not long ago should be a grave lesson on the dangers of putting one's faith in the riches of this world.

Yet, there are those who still subscribe to the "greed is good" fallacy. That's a recipe for disaster, for another global financial fiasco! How many more economic meltdowns do we really need to realize that *running a business or economy based on greed doesn't yield enduring profits?* God's way grounded in love is the only way of doing business that can yield reliable and everlasting profits. *God's way is built on helping, not hurting people.* Striving for enduring success, or hoping for lasting prosperity in any other way guarantees failure and disappointment.

"Instruct those who are rich in this present world not to be conceited or to **fix their hope** on the uncertainty of riches, but **on God**, who richly supplies us with all things to enjoy," the apostle Paul wrote, adding: "*Instruct them* to do good, to be **rich in good works,** to be **generous** and **ready to share**, storing up for themselves the **treasure of a good foundation for the future**, so that they may take hold of **that which is life indeed**" (1 Timothy 6:17-19, NASB, bold emphasis added).

What Money Can or Can't Buy

Certainly, "that which is life indeed" is not for sale. It cannot be purchased. Eternal life is a gift from God! Yes, it's true: there are many things money *cannot* buy. Your soul, for instance, is worth more than all the wealth of this world.

For sure, a soul stuck in sin lacks true freedom. Such a person lacks the ultimate in prosperity: eternal life with God in abundance. Indeed, wealth in this world *cannot* protect you from the law of sin and death or from the evil angels. *Only God can.* There can therefore be only one God in our lives.

Long ago, a sorcerer named Simon found out how unwise it can be to depend on wealth and not on God. He offered money to the apostles of Jesus

Christ in exchange for something that was not for sale. Simon sought to buy the power to lay hands on people so they'd receive the Holy Spirit!

But Peter rebuked the sorcerer: "Your money perish with you, *because you thought that the gift of God could be purchased with money!* You have neither part nor portion in this matter, for your heart is not right in the sight of God. Repent therefore of this your wickedness, and pray God if perhaps the thought of your heart may be forgiven you" (Acts 8:20-22, NKJV, emphasis added).

The forgiveness Peter spoke of above is something God freely gives to all who repent sincerely (see 1 John 1:9 and the chapter "Forgiveness: Guilty No More, Showing Others Mercy"). God offers forgiveness because out of love Jesus Christ paid for our sins at the cross. *We cannot buy God's forgiveness.* We either allow Jesus Christ to pay for our sin-debt or we pay for it with our own lives.

With great certainty, **money cannot buy salvation.** *Neither can money fill you up with the Holy Spirit.* Only God can! Our faith should therefore be in God, not in money or wealth (which God gives us anyway). Our faith entails a focus **not** on worldly or physical wealth but on God's everlasting kingdom and His righteousness (Matthew 6:33). In the kingdom of heaven, we definitely find eternal riches, permanent prosperity for our souls and many, many other great benefits – praise God!

A Focus on God: Everlasting Riches

A focus on God helps believers to stand strong no matter what challenges may come. Until Jesus Christ returns, believers must learn to cope with many challenges indeed. These may involve a revolving door of financial, emotional or physical problems. Nevertheless, we learn by God's grace to survive and thrive faithfully. With help from the Holy Spirit, we can be fruitful forever, not losing our integrity in a sinful world of trials, pains and sorrows.

Eventually, our faith in God is rewarded when the full extent of our riches in Jesus Christ is revealed: "that in the ages to come He might show the exceeding riches of His grace in His kindness toward us in Christ Jesus" (Ephesians 2:7, NKJV; see also 1 Corinthians 15:42-58 and Revelation 21:1-4).

For the time being, believers have to navigate with Godly wisdom the different challenges that do come. The economy may go bad. Jobs may disappear. Incomes may grow less, with profits dwindling for businesses. Nevertheless, we shall stand steadfast in faith, by God's grace, *knowing that our true riches, the real treasures of our prosperity in God never changes.* They are secured forever, invested in heaven and waiting for believers in God.

Additionally, in the present world, God can and will meet all of our needs. So fear not! Because He *is* Lord of heaven *and* earth, *God can weave the tapestry of economic, political and societal events to work in our favor.* Praise God, for He "causes all things to work together for good to those who love God, to those who are called according to *His* purpose" (Romans 8:28, NASB).

No Need to Worry

God indeed takes care of His very own children. So there is no need to worry. Believers are called to embrace these life-sustaining, encouraging words from Jesus Christ (Luke 12:22-24, NKJV): "Therefore I say to you, do not worry about your life, what you will eat; nor about the body, what you will put on. Life is more than food, and the body is more than clothing. Consider the ravens, for they neither sow nor reap, which have neither storehouse nor barn; and God feeds them. Of how much more value are you than the birds?"

We are of much greater value than the ravens. Such is our value to God that He redeemed us at great cost through His Son! *We are worth the life, the sacrifice of God's very own Son.* That is how valuable we are to our Heavenly Father. So, why worry?

Besides, which loving parent would starve his/her children? Or not give them the very best? If evil people know how to give good things to their children, we can only expect much more from an infinitely good and gracious God (see Matthew 7:11 and Luke 11:13). So, why worry? God knows what our needs are and can give them to us in abundance.

God Rewards the Faithful

However, the temptation to worry about our needs can be quite powerful. If we succumb to it, we can become too distracted from what should be our number one priority – God: *His Kingdom and His Righteousness.* That distraction can be costly and deadly.

Caution: our *worries can trick us into doing things that betray a lack of faith in God's ability to fulfill our needs.* For it is through faith that we please God: those who come "to God must believe that He is, and *that* He is a rewarder of those who diligently seek Him" (Hebrews 11:6, NKJV; see also Revelation 22:12).

Assuredly, the rewards for those who put their faith in God are immense, immeasurable and eternal. In Christ, we have everything, by God's grace. All that God has is ours, since we are joint heirs with Christ, heirs of God. All the riches of God belong to believers – praise God!

Worldly Wealth and Eternal Riches

We can have great worldly riches now but, more importantly, believers have everlasting prosperity. While worldly wealth is temporary, what we have in salvation through Jesus Christ is everlasting. And there is no reason we cannot *have both worldly wealth and eternal riches.* But we must *know which is more important,* which will last forever and which to focus on: *our treasures in heaven.* Indeed, our focus cannot be on the temporary. We must set our sights on the eternal: the kingdom of heaven.

As Jesus Christ noted: "But seek the kingdom of God, and all these things shall be added to you. Do not fear, little flock, for it is your Father's good pleasure to give you the kingdom. Sell what you have and give alms; provide yourselves money bags which do not grow old, a treasure in the heavens that does not fail, where no thief approaches nor moth destroys. For where your treasure is, there your heart will be also" (Luke 12:31-34, NKJV; see also Matthew 6).

Discussion Questions

1. What does it mean to gain riches in Jesus Christ? How does that relate to being rich toward God?

2. Why did Jesus Christ say we cannot worship God and money? And how does contentment demonstrate our dependence on God?

3. In what ways can you use your time, talent and treasures to serve God by helping people?

Chapter 20

Prayer

Prayer: Unlimited Access to Heaven

Highlights:

- Through prayer, we can cry out to God and receive help, anytime and anywhere.
- To have our prayers answered, however, we must follow specific directions from God.
- Prayer also involves listening to God – we just need to be tuned in to catch and embrace the divine message(s).

Two intercessors were working the late shift in the prayer room at the Brooklyn Tabernacle in New York. The night was almost like any other. A semblance of quiet prevailed in the near-empty building as the two took a short break. One intercessor then leaned back to rest where he sat. Suddenly, a dark presence came over him like a suffocating blanket. He could not move his limbs or scream out audibly for help. Conscious of his immediate surroundings though, he could still hear his prayer partner talking on the phone. Then a thought came to him. Using his inner voice, he cried out the name: JESUS! Instantly, the dark presence disappeared and he survived – praise God!

Answered Prayers and God's Voice

Praise God for His wonderful mercies and grace that night and always! I was that man, that intercessor. I thank God for rescuing me that night. I thank God also for countless other times of answered prayers. I praise the Lord for His matchless mercies, precious grace and endless love! God has been so good to me. Throughout the years, the Lord has been answering my many, many prayers. Prayer certainly works. *Calling on the name of Jesus Christ works!* God listens for sure to the cries of His children – praise the Lord!

Not only does He listen, but He also talks to us. We just need to be tuned in to catch His voice through Jesus Christ who *is* the Word of God (see John 1). But not everyone can hear the Lord's voice: "*My sheep hear My voice*, and I know them, and *they follow Me*; and I give eternal life to them, and *they will never perish*; and no one will snatch them out of My hand. *My Father, who has given them to Me, is greater than all*; and no one is able to snatch *them* out of the Father's hand. *I and the Father are one*" (John 10:27-30, NASB, bold emphasis added; see also John 8:47).

Decidedly, there is potential for confusion in the area of hearing God clearly. The Lord however is *not* behind confusion (1 Corinthians 14:33), so be cautious. There are many fakers out there. Unscrupulous, these are false messengers pretending to be from God. "For such are false apostles, deceitful workers, transforming themselves into apostles of Christ. And no wonder! *For Satan himself transforms himself into an angel of light.* Therefore it is no great thing if *his ministers also transform themselves into ministers of righteousness*, whose end will be according to their works" (2 Corinthians 11:13-15, NKJV, emphasis added).

So watch out. Helped by the Holy Spirit, you can use the Holy Bible to prayerfully verify what you see or hear or experience. You don't want to be misled. You certainly don't want to make wrong choices. If what you see, hear or experience contradicts the Bible, run for your life. And pray always for God to help you hear His voice clearly.

Defeating Evil Schemes

Significantly, non-believers are particularly vulnerable to devilish schemes. If you are not saved (if you are not a true believer in God), your situation is dangerous. John 10:27-30 quoted earlier does not apply to you because you are not of the sheepfold of Jesus Christ. As Jesus stated: "My sheep hear my voice, and I know them, and they follow me" (John 10:27, ESV). Moreover: "Whoever is of God hears the words of God. The reason why you do not hear them is that you are not of God" (John 8:47, ESV).

For your immediate protection, you are better off making your peace with God right now, if you are not saved! (Please see the last three paragraphs of this chapter for a helpful prayer – it is located before this chapter's footnote – and then come back here to continue reading.) Once saved, by God's grace, you come to stand on a stronger foundation as you are strengthened by the Holy Spirit. You are therefore better equipped to recognize and resist the deceptions of the devil. And God indeed helps you to defeat evil, enabling you to overcome sin and death forever.

Able to Do Exceedingly Great Things

As noted earlier, a great prayer point here is to constantly ask for God's help to hear His voice clearly and block out all the fakers. The Lord certainly enables us to hear, understand *and obey* Him. And we do need God's help to obey His commandments centered in love. With the Holy Spirit empowering us, we most certainly can.

Yes, we surely are able to do exceedingly great things in the Lord. "Most assuredly, I say to you, he who believes in Me, the works that I do he will do also; and **greater *works* than these he will do,** because I go to My Father. And whatever you ask in My name, that I will do, that the Father may be glorified in the Son. If you ask anything in My name, I will do *it*," the Son of God told His early disciples in a promise that applies to all of God's children today (John 14:12-14, NKJV, bold emphasis added)

In What Manner to Pray

Through prayer, in the name of Jesus Christ, we can come to God with all of our requests – praise God! Indeed, when we pray, we get to actually communicate with the Lord of heaven and earth. How amazing is that!

In communicating with God, we certainly can learn to pray better. We can learn from what Jesus Christ taught His early disciples. Jesus taught them in what manner to pray as quoted below (Matthew 6:9-13, NKJV):

"Our Father in heaven,
Hallowed be Your name.
Your kingdom come.
Your will be done
On earth as *it is* in heaven.
Give us this day our daily bread.
And forgive us our debts,
As we forgive our debtors.
And do not lead us into temptation,
But deliver us from the evil one.
For Yours is the kingdom and the power and the glory forever.
Amen."

Getting Help Quickly

When we pray, we can stay connected with heaven and can get help quickly. I know. I have been there. *In my experience, the help we get from God is one that nobody else can give us.* I thank God for being there to help me countless times. God has helped me numerous times when aid could come from nowhere else. Only You, *Lord*, can do it! To You belong all the honor, all the glory and all the praises – hallelujah!

We praise God for Jesus Christ! His atonement for sin enables us to have peace with God. His sacrifice thus enables our access to God. "For through Him we both have access by one Spirit to the Father" (Ephesians 2:18, NKJV). Therefore we have no need to fear and can confidently approach God. "Let us therefore come boldly unto the throne of grace, that we may obtain mercy, and find grace to help in time of need" (Hebrews 4:16, KJV).

Besides, we don't have to pay when we come to God for help. When we call out to our Heavenly Father, the call is free to us, with unlimited access. Jesus Christ has already covered the cost by dying on the cross for our sins – praise God! This is real, truly unlimited access.

The access believers have to God is quite amazing. People typically don't have that type of access to rulers on earth. Presidents, kings, queens and other rulers are rarely accessible. But a gracious and good God, more powerful than anyone else, opens up access to heaven readily through Jesus Christ. Praise God!

In Jesus Christ, moreover, we have an everlasting High Priest helping us in heaven (see Hebrews 7, 8 and 9). "But now He has obtained a more excellent ministry, by as much as He is also the mediator of a better covenant, which has been enacted on better promises" (Hebrews 8:6, NASB).

Access for Nonbelievers?

Importantly, access to the kingdom of heaven, although unlimited because of Jesus Christ, is for the saved. Access is for believers in God. These are people with their names written in the Book of Life in heaven.

Note: those desiring salvation, for sure, can reach out to God too. The Lord certainly hears the cries of repentant souls. These are *people sincerely seeking God*, desiring escape from the clutches of sin and death.

If you are not saved, you can simply cry out now: ***Lord, please help me!*** God hears that plea. The Lord will never cast out anyone that comes to Him (see John 6:37). So pray expectantly.

Great Power in the Name of Jesus

Our amazing God loves us deeply. He makes it possible for us to cry out to Him when we need help. As I discovered that night in Brooklyn, at the moment of our deepest desperation, we don't even need to be able to talk.

Audibly or inwardly, we can cry out to the name that God has ordained to be above all others: "so that at the name of Jesus EVERY KNEE WILL BOW, of those who are in heaven and on earth and under the earth" (Philippians 2:10, NASB).

And it certainly doesn't matter at what time of the day or night we need help. We can call on the name of God anytime: morning, noon, evening or night. It doesn't matter how big or small the problem may be. It matters not whether our situation seems impossible. God *is* able to meet us at the point of our need. Just cry out to God in the name of Jesus Christ!

Do You Want Your Prayers Answered?

A word of caution though: while we may boldly come to the throne of grace, there are guidelines we must follow. For our prayers to be answered, we must **come to God in humility**. For instance, there is this parable that Jesus told. It was about two men who went up to the temple one day to pray. One of them, a Pharisee, "stood and prayed thus with himself, 'God, I thank You that I am not like other men – extortioners, unjust, adulterers, or even as this tax collector. I fast twice a week; I give tithes of all that I possess'" (Luke 18:11-12, NKJV).

The other, a tax collector "standing afar off, would not so much as raise his eyes to heaven, but beat his breast, saying, 'God, be merciful to me a sinner!' I tell you, this man went down to his house justified rather than the other; for *everyone who exalts himself will be humbled, and he who humbles himself will be exalted*" (Luke 18:13-14, NKJV, emphasis added).

There are indeed crucial rules for effective prayer – *humility* being one and **repentance for sin** being another. And as the Psalmist noted: "If I regard wickedness in my heart, The Lord will not hear" (Psalm 66:18, NASB). Our sins need to be confessed and forsaken before God so they don't hinder our prayers. Furthermore, we must be **sincere** when we come to God, relying on the **Holy Spirit** (the Spirit of truth) so we can worship God **in spirit** and **in truth** (see John 4:23-24, John 14:17 and John 16:13).

In addition to humility, repentance, the Holy Spirit and sincerity, we need unwavering faith for success in prayer. We must avoid doubts. "But he must *ask in faith without any doubting*, for the one who doubts is like the surf of the sea, driven and tossed by the wind" (James 1:6, NASB, bold emphasis added).

Praying without Ceasing and Counteracting Temptation

Furthermore, we are to offer **continuous prayer**. Indeed, we are to "pray without ceasing" (1 Thessalonians 5:17, ESV). There are so many things we need God's help for in this continuously perilous world. The Lord's wisdom, guidance, strength and comfort is required constantly.

In addition, the temptation to sin can come ceaselessly from all corners. Believers (and non-believers) are persistently bombarded with distractions and diversions from God's way. We need God's help to find His way and to stay on it.

Critically, prayer helps us to counteract temptation and to stay on course. As Jesus commanded: "*Watch and pray that you may not enter into temptation.* The spirit indeed is willing, but the flesh is weak" (Mark 14:38, ESV, bold emphasis added).

Besides, God watches out for us: "No temptation has overtaken you that is not common to man. God is faithful, and he will not let you be tempted beyond your ability, but with the temptation he will also provide the way of escape, that you may be able to endure it" (1 Corinthians 10:13, ESV). Praise God!

Motives for Prayer

We must ensure, moreover, that we have *proper motives* for our prayers. "You ask and do not receive, because you ask with wrong motives, so that you may spend *it* on your pleasures" (James 4:3, NASB).

Note that a misreading of James 4:3 may give the wrong impression that God does not want us to have fun. Of course, He does! "You make known to me the path of life; in your presence there is fullness of joy; at your right hand are pleasures forevermore," wrote King David about God (Psalm 16:11, ESV). God wants us to *have fun the right way*. The wrong way brings sorrows!

Our prayers, basically, must line up with God's law, His righteousness grounded in love. At the core of our compliance with God's commandments stands love. So what type of love do we truly have if our prayers are focused solely on God blessing us? What of those suffering around us? *Do we intend to be a blessing to them when we are blessed?* When prayer is done right, God moves mightily to answer. He desires to bless us – so that we can be a blessing to others – as we demonstrate our love for Him by loving others.

God Desires the Best for Us

Our heavenly Father God, the Lord of heaven and earth, desires the best for us because He loves us. We need to seek Him and present our requests. We need to *come to God in humility, repentance, sincerity, faith and selflessness.* And *aided by the Holy Spirit,* we are to *"watch and pray" to God continuously.* When we approach God the right way, we can receive from Him great treasures, many good gifts. Our gracious and good God has endless streams of blessings for us – praise the Lord!

"And I tell you, ask, and it will be given to you; seek, and you will find; knock, and it will be opened to you. For everyone who asks receives, and the one who seeks finds, and to the one who knocks it will be opened. What father among you, if his son asks for a fish, will instead of a fish give him a serpent; or if he asks for an egg, will give him a scorpion? If you then, who are evil, know how to give good gifts to your children, *how much more will the heavenly Father give the Holy Spirit to those who ask him*" (Luke 11:9-13, ESV, emphasis added).

The Greatest Giver of Good Gifts

God is the ultimate giver of good gifts. No one can out-give God. If you are not saved, God desires that you come to Him to receive good gifts. So come to God now. He will receive you gladly. In fact, there is joy in heaven at one sinner that repents (see Luke 15:7). That's how important you are to God. **The Lord loves you!**

So don't delay. Come to God now for true love. He'll give you joy and peace. *God will forgive your sins no matter how bad you think they are.* You just need to repent. The Lord God will give you rest from all your burdens. You don't need to carry all that pain, hurt or problems anymore. Give it to God. He will handle it. God can help you to become better and burden-free. So make the right move now to embrace God's amazing love and great power.

Please say this prayer now: "*Dear God, please come into my life. I admit I am a sinner – please forgive me. I acknowledge that Jesus Christ died for my sins and rose from the dead by the power of the Holy Spirit. I accept Jesus Christ as my Lord and Savior. Please fill me up with the Holy Spirit. Help me to do Your will and succeed forever. In Jesus name I pray: Amen!*"

The above is one prayer that God readily answers, if the repentance is sincere. That prayer opens the door for you to be reconciled with God and to have a relationship with Him – it facilitates your access to heaven. Besides, when you ask God to fill you up with the Holy Spirit, you are asking for everything that you need to succeed for eternity.

With the Holy Spirit empowering you, and helping you in prayer, you get to enjoy the endless benefits reserved for those God favors through Jesus Christ. So pray expectantly as you watch the blessings of God increase and abound in your life. Enjoy!

Footnote on Prayer

- One of the most amazing experiences in my life occurred at a Tuesday Night Prayer Meeting at the Brooklyn Tabernacle in New York many years ago. Pastor Jim Cymbala typically describes the prayer meeting as the most important in the church, even more so than the Sunday services. That night, as the meeting progressed towards the end, a call was made for those needing specific prayers (as per the 'altar call') to come upfront to the altar. Few people went. I was one of them.

- After we were prayed for collectively, I felt led strongly to ask the gentleman standing behind me in the dimly-lit auditorium to pray specifically for me. I did. I'm glad I did! The very first words from the man addressed an issue that had bothered me because of wrong teachings elsewhere that I knew, by God's grace, to be wrong teachings. The man said: "You have the Holy Spirit in you". Wow – praise God! You have no idea how much relief and reassurance I received that night from the Lord, delivered through the mouth of a complete stranger!

- *I had never met the man before that night.* I was quite new to the church so there was no way he could have known my story. I was very withdrawn personally and would rather not talk about my personal issues. So there was no way he could have heard the matter from somebody else. God was simply using a complete stranger to minister to me. After the man prayed for me, I was so impressed that I asked for his name. He said: Kenneth Ware! Later on, I found out that he was the well-respected overseeing pastor for the Prayer Band ministry at the church, which I later served in. Praise God! My Lord is so wonderful.

Discussion Questions

---

1. Are there requirements for your prayers to be answered by God? Why
    is humility, sincerity, repentance or faith important in prayer? What
    of the right motives – how is that different from wrong motives for
    prayer?

2. What are the great works believers will do as noted in John 14:12-14?
    How is love involved in the great works? How does reading Ephesians
    2:10 and Matthew 3:8 affect your perspective?

3. Why is it problematic to pray for something that is not in the will of
    God and how can we hear God clearly?

Chapter 21

Praise Power

Praise Power: Praising God to Prevail

Highlights:

- God deserves our praises for all that He has done, is doing and is going to do in our lives.
- There is tremendous power in praising God – it shows a heart of gratitude and demonstrates faith which God notices and rewards greatly.
- God responds to our praises in ways that are empowering to believers, encouraging even more praise.

Paul and Silas were caught in a very bad situation. Beaten and imprisoned for the gospel of Jesus Christ, the two refused to surrender to the dictates of their depressing conditions. They did not sit quietly, sulking and sorrowful. Instead they did something quite surprising. Well, surprising to those who do not understand the power of praising God.

"But about midnight Paul and Silas were praying and singing hymns of praise to God, and the prisoners were listening to them; and suddenly there came a great earthquake, so that the foundations of the prison house were shaken; and immediately all the doors were opened and everyone's chains were unfastened. When the jailer awoke and saw the prison doors opened, he drew his sword and was about to kill himself, supposing that the prisoners had escaped. But Paul cried out with a loud voice, saying, 'Do not harm yourself, for we are all here'" (Acts 16:25-28, NASB)!

Thankfulness: Praising God No Matter What Happens

Both men had maintained a consistent attitude of acknowledging God regardless of the depths of their *horrible but temporary* conditions. Their unwavering faith resulted in divine intervention on their behalf. There are definitely great benefits for God's children who consistently maintain an attitude of acknowledging, worshiping and praising God no matter what happens.

From an eternity perspective, believers are to regard temporary circumstances as, well, temporary! Those circumstances, no matter how difficult or bad, cannot last forever. God **will not** allow believers to suffer forever. So the temporary should *not* affect our thankfulness towards an eternal God who offers us *great, good and everlasting benefits*. These benefits eventually will far outweigh, indeed override our sufferings or difficulties in this passing world (see Romans 8:18) – praise God!

Certainly, we are to "give thanks in all circumstances; for this is the will of God in Christ Jesus for you" (1 Thessalonians 5:18, ESV). For believers, our thankfulness comes from a mindset that embraces and appreciates God's salvation plan. It's a perspective that operates under the power of God's love, enabling us to love others, transforming us and the world for good. God's power overcomes all adversities, obstacles or challenges in our path to becoming more loving, regardless of how bad or big the problems may be. Believers are victorious, successful and secured forever – praise God!

As believers, we have access to the most powerful force in the universe. Like Paul and Silas, we can even afford to be generous to our jail keepers. We can afford to be gracious to those who seek our ruin when the power of God gives us victory over them. When the jailer in the story above realized that the two men had not escaped, he "fell down trembling before Paul and Silas" (Acts 16:29, NKJV).

A Question worth Asking

The trembling man then posed a question that you should be asking, if you are not yet a child of God: "Sirs, what must I do to be saved?" And they told him: "Believe in the Lord Jesus, and you will be saved, you and your household" (Acts 16:30-31, NASB: read the rest of the story in the Bible).

The path to salvation today entails that you accept the sacrifice that Jesus Christ made to atone for sin. You need to "confess with your mouth that Jesus is Lord and believe in your heart that God raised him from the dead, you will be saved" (Romans 10:9, ESV). Indeed, all who call on the name of the Lord will be saved (Romans 10:12-14 and Joel 2:32). We cannot but be grateful to God and glorify His name! Praise the Lord! Hallelujah!

Gratitude to God

Our gratitude to God comes because of what He has done, and continues to do through Jesus Christ and the Holy Spirit. The Son of God died for our sins and was raised through the power of the Holy Spirit. Enabling us to be born again, this same Spirit of God dwells within believers (see John 3:3-6, Romans 8:9-11 and Acts 11:16). The Spirit enables us to live the new life as God's children for eternity in accordance with His commandments. This new life elicits *an attitude of gratitude* in us who are enjoying the benefits of what God has done, and is doing to build us up into the image of His Son.

An attitude of gratitude can take believers up to *an altitude* far over and above whatever may be trying to hold us down, or drag us backwards. Underscored by faith in God, this attitude and altitude promotes a mindset of acknowledging, worshiping and praising the Lord regardless of our current situations. It's a perspective, an outlook that is driven and reinforced by God's love evident in our lives, with clear changes and improvements in us. We do have great testimonies, much to thank God for – praise the Lord! What a great blessing and privilege to have experiences to thank God for! May the name of the Lord be exalted forever – amen!

Beauty, Joy and Praise

Our faith in God certainly does produce tangible results. Our ultimate hope is in God's unwavering faithfulness and matchless grace, providing us with great eternal benefits through Jesus Christ, our Lord and Savior. The good news is that those benefits can include "beauty for ashes, the oil of joy for mourning" and "the garment of praise for the spirit of heaviness". And these come so that we "might be called trees of righteousness, the planting of the Lord, that he might be glorified" (Isaiah 61:3, KJV). Praise the Lord!

Believers are grateful for God's power in love enabling us to be fruitful in good works, thereby glorifying God (see 2 Timothy 1:7, Ephesians 2:10, John 15:8, Galatians 5:22-23, Matthew 5:16 and John 15:1-7). With God's presence in our lives, we get to exchange the bad for the good. God enables us to experience the joy of salvation (see Psalm 51:12). Indeed: "You have made known to me the ways of life; You will make me full of joy in Your presence" (Acts 2:28, NKJV; see also Psalm 16:11). Reinforcing our faith, God's presence ensures believers attain victories upon victories over all adversaries and adversities, including the final enemy: death – praise God!

God Helps Us Prevail Over Our Trials

Categorically, there is no power greater than God. The Lord God is able to subdue all of our enemies and deliver us from all evils or afflictions. "Many are the afflictions of the righteous, but the LORD delivers him out of them all (Psalm 34:19, ESV).

Because of His love for us, God has given His Son Jesus to ensure that we succeed for eternity. Therefore, no matter what may come against us in life, believers are assured of victory. "And we know that God causes all things to work together for good to those who love God, to those who are called according to *His* purpose" (Romans 8:28, NASB).

Eventually, by God's grace those saved (believers) will survive the second death and the impending destruction of this passing world. Beyond survival, believers get to inherit the new world, the new heaven and earth, in a new age to be ushered in when Jesus Christ returns. The dead in Christ will be resurrected, and all believers will inherit a new, spiritual and incorruptible body forever – praise the Lord God!

Glory: A Great Inheritance

The knowledge of our ultimate inheritance in God gives believers a transforming and triumphant perspective on our current challenges or difficulties. We have the eternity perspective, our mindset transformed to one of intense faith. We see where God brought us from, and where He is taking us to: from glory to glory onto the kingdom of heaven. We cannot but acknowledge what a great lot we have to thank God for.

Even if we get thrown in jail like Paul and Silas, as believers, we are *by God's grace* still able to keep acknowledging, worshipping and praising God. We cannot hold back the showers of praises flowing from our grateful lips. Because of our transformed mindset focused on the kingdom of God and His righteousness, we can stand unshakable regardless of the situation.

As a result, even in suffering, sorrow, pain or prison we can boldly shout and sing: "Hallelujah anyhow!" And as the apostle Paul noted: "For I consider that the sufferings of this present time are not worthy *to be compared with the glory which shall be revealed in us*" (Romans 8:18, NKJV). Praise the Lord!

A Mindset of Intense Faith

When operating in this renewed mindset of intense faith, of acknowledging, worshiping and praising God regardless of the situation, we stand in a supernatural zone. It is a divine place of supreme power and provision that is called up on our behalf by God's grace.

As Paul and Silas can attest to, God indeed responds to our praises! And as King David wrote in Psalm 22:3 (KJV): "But thou art holy, O thou that inhabitest the praises of Israel"! We likewise should expect God to inhabit our praises. And with God's presence in our lives, we are joyous and victorious for now and forever – praise the Lord!

Indeed, as the evidence of God's favor is demonstrated, we like the writer of Psalm 28:6-7 (NKJV) can loudly and boldly proclaim:

> "Blessed *be* the LORD,
> Because He has heard the voice of my supplications!
> The LORD *is* my strength and my shield;
> My heart trusted in Him, and I am helped;
> Therefore my heart greatly rejoices,
> And with my song I will praise Him."

Moreover, like King David in Psalm 103:1-5 (NKJV), we can joyously say and sing with a heart of gratitude:

> "Bless the LORD, O my soul;
> And all that is within me, *bless* His holy name!
> Bless the LORD, O my soul,
> And forget not all His benefits:
> Who forgives all your iniquities,
> Who heals all your diseases,
> Who redeems your life from destruction,
> Who crowns you with lovingkindness and tender mercies,
> Who satisfies your mouth with good *things,*
> *So that* your youth is renewed like the eagle's."

Amen and amen! *All praises are to the Most High and Holy God!* Thank You Lord God for Jesus Christ! Thank You for the Holy Spirit! Thank You for salvation! Thank You for the new heavens and the new earth! Thank You for the new incorruptible spiritual body! Thank You for eternal life in the kingdom of heaven! Hallelujah! All praises are due to You, Heavenly Father! You deserve more than our praises! Thank You Lord Jesus!

Discussion Questions

1. Why do we need to praise God? Why does the Creator of the universe in whose image we are made deserve our continued gratitude and praise?

2. Why does an attitude of praising God regardless of the situation yield such great results as seen in the lives of Paul, Silas and other servants of God? What do you think of Psalm 22:3-5: what lessons can you learn here?

3. How can you come to have that attitude of praising, worshiping and acknowledging God continuously in your life regardless of the situation?

Chapter 22

Healing

Healing: Succor for the Soul

Highlights:

- God provides salvation for lost souls, offering everlasting relief and redemption from the curse and afflictions of sin and death.
- The redemptive process starts when we are saved, bringing **healing** for all of our inward and outward afflictions **ultimately**.
- We can all get permanent succor for the soul, everlasting freedom from the afflictions, the troubles in this world that can produce so much sorrow for even the strongest.

When they heard that Jesus was passing by, the two blind men cried out: "Have mercy on us, O Lord, Son of David"! Although the crowd following Jesus warned them to be quiet, the blind men persisted, repeating their cries for help. Stopping, Jesus asked what they wanted him to do for them. "Lord, that our eyes may be opened," they answered. "So Jesus had compassion and touched their eyes. And immediately their eyes received sight, and they followed Him" (Matthew 20:29-34, NKJV). Praise the Lord God!

Permanent Relief from All Afflictions

The Bible is interspersed with the many miracles of Jesus Christ. He healed the sick. He drove out demons. With little, He fed thousands. He turned water into wine, even walking on water. He calmed a storm, rebuking the wind. For sure, these and others are great miracles. Yet, they are surpassed by probably the greatest miracles of all: the sacrifice at the cross and the resurrection of Jesus Christ.

Through Jesus Christ, thankfully, we get to overcome the fallout from Adam's fall (see Genesis 3). No longer do humans have to succumb to the curse of sin and death – praise God! Through the Lord Jesus Christ, God amazingly demonstrates His matchless love, mercy and grace, offering salvation to lost souls, and permanent relief from all afflictions.

"For if by the transgression of the one, death reigned through the one, much more those who receive the abundance of grace and of the gift of righteousness will reign in life through the One, Jesus Christ. So then as through one transgression there resulted condemnation to all men, even so through one act of righteousness there resulted justification of life to all men" (Romans 5:17-18, NASB). Those saved get eternal life with freedom ultimately from all diseases, pains and sorrows – praise God!

As the Prophet Isaiah foretold, in a prophecy that has come to pass through Jesus Christ (Isaiah 53:4-6, NKJV):

> "Surely He has borne our griefs
> And carried our sorrows;
> Yet we esteemed Him stricken,
> Smitten by God, and afflicted.
> But He was wounded for our transgressions,
> He was bruised for our iniquities;
> The chastisement for our peace was upon Him,
> And *by His stripes we are healed.*
> *All we like sheep have gone astray*;
> We have turned, every one, to his own way;
> And *the Lord has laid on Him the iniquity of us all*" (emphasis added).

Much More Than Physical Healing

At the cross, Jesus Christ miraculously exchanged sin and its consequences for everlasting life available to all who believe in God. He took on our troubles: griefs, afflictions and iniquities. They were all overcome at the cross – praise God!

The obvious question then is: if that is so, *why then do people still fall sick and die,* even believers? Yes, even those who have accepted God's salvation plan? While the power of miraculous healing of bodily diseases is available *through* and *to* the children of God, there is *much more than physical healing* available to believers.

The ultimate goal of salvation is not to patch up the battered, corrupted body inherited by humans from the *first man (Adam)*. God plans to replace it with a transformed, incorruptible body fashioned after the *second Man (Jesus)*. Believers will be getting a disease-free heavenly body eventually – praise God! "The first man was of the earth, made of dust; the second Man is the Lord from heaven. As was the man of dust, so also are those who are made of dust; and as is the heavenly Man, so also are those who are heavenly. And as we have borne the image of the man of dust, we shall also bear the image of the heavenly Man" (1 Corinthians 15:47-49, NKJV).

Moreover: "So is it with the resurrection of the dead. What is sown is perishable; what is raised is imperishable. It is sown in dishonor; it is raised in glory. It is sown in weakness; it is raised in power. It is sown a natural body; it is raised a spiritual body. If there is a natural body, there is also a spiritual body" (1 Corinthians 15:42-44, ESV).

The full realization of the believer's transformation occurs when Jesus Christ returns: "But our citizenship is in heaven, and from it we await a Savior, the Lord Jesus Christ, who will transform our lowly body to be like his glorious body, by the power that enables him even to subject all things to himself" (Philippians 3:20-21, ESV). Praise God, and amen!

Overcoming a Body of Sin and Death

Although the soul that sins is condemned to die, believers get eternal life and will inherit a spiritual body like that of Jesus Christ. The Son of God lives forever – so will those identified with Him (believers). However, those unsaved (nonbelievers) are sadly stuck with the body inherited from Adam, a body of sin, sorrow, disease and death.

Note though that before Jesus Christ returns and believers get the heavenly body, *we all must still* contend with the faults, frailties and failures of the body inherited from Adam. Believers though have a divine advantage. We get God's comfort through the Holy Spirit working within us to ease the burdens of our presently weak bodies – thank God!

Unfortunately, if you are not saved, you miss out greatly. You are stuck in sin without succor from God. You'll miss the great benefits of eternal life with God. To avoid that dismal fate, you should make your peace with God immediately. *You can get saved right now, and be set free from sin and death.* Why be stuck with corruption when you can get perfection? Why settle for the body inherited from Adam when you can get a perfect upgrade? Yes, an eternally superior upgrade through Jesus Christ, the Son of God! Praise the Lord!

Victory in the Resurrection and God's Power to Help Us

It is important to note that while on this earth with the body inherited from Adam, we may fall sick or even die. God, at His discretion and infinite wisdom, may decide to provide healing or postpone our death. But if we are *believers in God,* and we do die, we *are sure to be resurrected* and escape the second death when Jesus Christ returns (see John 5:25-29 and Revelation 20:6).

Significantly, the Sovereign Lord may decide not to provide immediate healing for a specific condition as occurred in the case of the apostle Paul. In other words, when bodily healing is not given, God provides the means for believers to *cope with and rise above the condition.* And the condition *cannot* last forever for believers anyway – praise the Lord!

As Paul noted concerning his condition mentioned above: "So to keep me from becoming conceited because of the surpassing greatness of the revelations, a thorn was given me in the flesh, a messenger of Satan to harass me, to keep me from becoming conceited. Three times I pleaded with the Lord about this, that it should leave me. But he said to me, 'My grace is sufficient for you, for my power is made perfect in weakness.' Therefore I will boast all the more gladly of my weaknesses, so that the power of Christ may rest upon me" (2 Corinthians 12:7-9, ESV).

Succor by God's Grace

For those who may have to go through many afflictions or difficulties, God's help is invaluable. By God's grace, believers get the succor, the comfort to *go on* and *grow through* such terrible conditions. Regardless of the situation, the Lord provides divine peace. Surely, "the peace of God, which passeth all understanding, shall keep your hearts and minds through Christ Jesus" (Philippians 4:7, KJV). It is a promise of peace to believers who place their trust and hope in God.

Regardless of the extremities of the adversities, believers have an immense capacity to cope and thrive as empowered by God – praise the Lord! We can remain steadfast in faith, by God's grace, no matter what happens. Strengthened by the Holy Spirit, believers have boundless hope and joy in God's salvation.

Besides, our struggles are only for a time and season, whereas God's favor in our lives lasts forever – praise the Lord! "…His favor is for life; Weeping may endure for a night, But joy comes in the morning" (Psalm 30:5, NKJV). Hallelujah!

The Complete Restorative Work by Jesus Christ

By the grace of God, the healing available to the children of God is ultimately the complete redemptive, restorative work by Jesus Christ. It is a process of restoration that culminates in His second coming to usher in a new age. The book of Revelation records what the promise and reality of that new age would be like. There will be no more death, sorrows or tears (see Revelation 21:4). It would be a new and vastly better world. And believers get to live in it, forever – praise the Lord!

What awaits believers is the ultimate work of re-creation, regeneration, where all those who are saved will forever discard the disease-prone, sin-tormented body inherited from Adam. Believers will have a new, spiritual body – just like Jesus Christ's: free of sin, diseases and death – no corruption. The coming experience is beyond description, beyond the marvelous, beyond anything we have ever imagined. Praise God!

Because of God's love, mercy and grace, believers will come to live forever in the presence of almighty God. And in His presence, as the Psalmist wrote, "is fulness of joy; at thy right hand there are pleasures for evermore" (Psalm

16:11, KJV – see also the chapters: "Hope: Faith in God for a New and Better Life" and "New World: No More Sorrow").

All Praises to God for His Wonderful Works

Thank You Lord for Your limitless love, endless mercies and matchless grace! Thank You for joy and complete healing! Thank You for salvation! Thank You for Your endless love demonstrated through Jesus Christ even while we were yet sinners. Thank You for peace, success and prosperity! Thank You for unmerited favor! Thank You for life eternal! Thank You for the love that You have shown us over the years and continue to show us. I love You, Lord. Thank You! I am forever grateful.

Hallelujah! Hallelujah! Hallelujah!

Discussion Questions

1. What is the soul and why does the Bible state that the soul that sins shall die? What is the source of our afflictions, and how is that related to sin and death?

2. How can our soul be redeemed from death? What of our spirit and body – how are they all connected and contaminated by sin?

3. What is the ultimate healing or redemption available through the sacrifice by Jesus Christ at the cross?

Chapter 23

Protection

Protection for Eternal Life

Highlights:

- God offers us protection from seen and unseen dangers in a world full of sin and nasty characters capable of doing us grave harm.
- Humans are opposed and oppressed by spiritual forces of evil with great powers but God is more powerful.
- God is the key to human survival: the Lord's protection provides assurance to believers of eternal victory over all enemies.

No one could subdue him. They tried binding him with chains and shackles, but the man tore up the chains and shattered the shackles. Day and night always, he lived in the mountains and among the tombs, crying out and slashing himself with stones. Then he met the Son of God. During that encounter, Jesus asked the demon-possessed man: "What is your name?" The man replied: "My name is Legion; for we are many" (Mark 5:8-9, NASB).

Superior Power

Few or many, the demons did not stand a chance. Confronted by *the* superior power of Jesus Christ, they succumbed, expelled from the harried man. The Son of God had spoken. Jesus had given the order! Then people came and "saw the one *who had been* demon-possessed and had the legion, sitting and clothed and in his right mind. And they were afraid" (Mark 5:15, NKJV). God be praised!

Afterwards, Jesus told the man: "Go home to your friends, and tell them what great things the Lord has done for you, and how He has had compassion on you" (Mark 5:19, NKJV). That compassion, that mercy is available to everyone today. The possessed man's story illustrates what may not be obvious: there are spiritual forces of wickedness, agents of darkness all around us. They can steal our joy, shatter our peace and damage our lives.

Evil is real. Evil beings: the devil and demons (as well as evil humans) are real. Without God's help, we stand exposed like sitting ducks. Without God's protection, we are hopeless and helpless against the onslaught of spiritual forces of wickedness that can attack us anytime either directly or through other humans. God is our strength, the key to our protection and survival! We need God's full armor!

The Whole Armor of God

"Finally, be strong in the Lord and in the strength of His might. Put on the full armor of God, so that you will be able to stand firm against the schemes of the devil. For **our struggle is not against flesh and blood**, but against the rulers, against the powers, against the world forces of this darkness, against the spiritual *forces* of wickedness in the heavenly *places*" (Ephesians 6:10-12, NASB, bold emphasis added). We can stand firm because *nothing* and *no one* can overcome God's armor.

As helpfully noted by the apostle Paul, the "full armor of God" has many components: "Stand therefore, having your loins girt about with **truth**, and having on the breastplate of **righteousness**; And your feet shod with the preparation of the **gospel of peace**; Above all, taking the **shield of faith**, wherewith ye shall be able to quench all the fiery darts of the wicked. And take **the helmet of salvation**, and the **sword of the Spirit**, which is **the word of God**: Praying always with all **prayer** and supplication in the Spirit, and watching thereunto with all perseverance and supplication for all saints..." (Ephesians 6:14-18, KJV, bold emphasis added).

Protection against all Powerful Enemies

Equipped with the complete armor of God, believers have the ultimate defense against all dangers, all evils and all enemies. That includes demons or humans under evil influences or control. The fallen angels especially pose a peculiar threat because they are not usually visible to the physical eye. Fallen in rebellion against God, they are powerful beings who have no love for humans. In fact, they mean us harm, grave harm.

But under God's protection, we can stand firm and secure against all adversaries, no matter how big or bad. Greater than all, the Lord God is our salvation from all evils, our strength and refuge. As King David wrote: "In God is my salvation and my glory: the rock of my strength, and my refuge, is in God" (Psalm 62:7, KJV). Moreover: "God is our refuge and strength, a very present help in trouble" (Psalm 46:1, KJV).

Because God has superior power, He can rescue and protect us when trouble comes. But we must first submit to God. We must submit to the Lord's way. We need to come under His law grounded in love as enabled by Jesus Christ working in our hearts through the Holy Spirit.

"Submit therefore to God. Resist the devil and he will flee from you. Draw near to God and He will draw near to you. Cleanse your hands, you sinners; and purify your hearts, you double-minded" (James 4:7-8, NASB; see also Romans 5:5). It is crucial to understand that to win against forces of evil, *we must first submit to God*. Otherwise, we would stand exposed, helpless and hopeless.

Accept or Reject God's Protection?

It's a choice. We can embrace God or reject His protection. If we do reject God, we would stand vulnerable to the schemes of the devil. When we do accept God's way, however, we stand strong, powerful. Nothing can overcome us permanently. God enables us through the Holy Spirit to stay in His will, walking in His way grounded in love. In God, we have the most powerful being in the world helping us – praise the Lord!

We must however *not see God's protection as a license to sin*. We cannot risk reverting to a lifestyle of sinning by walking in our own way: in malice, greed and arrogance. A lifestyle of sinning can leave us exposed to seen and unseen dangers, compromising our protection.

But by walking in the power of God's Holy Spirit, we stand protected. The Spirit enables us, enhances us to resist the temptation to sin. And if we do fall into sin, God is very forgiving, as long as we acknowledge our wrongs. We must confess and repent. "If we say we have no sin, we deceive ourselves, and the truth is not in us. If we confess our sins, he is faithful and just to forgive us our sins and to cleanse us from all unrighteousness. If we say we have not sinned, we make him a liar, and his word is not in us" (1 John 1:8-10, ESV).

An Old Human Disease: Sin

Sin or disobedience to God is an old human disease. It's driven largely by hatred (malice), selfishness (greed) and arrogance (pride). It is contrary to God's way of love, giving and humility.

Sin, sadly, has shortchanged our lives. Because our first parents gave in to the wiles of the devil and succumbed to the pull of sin, they disobeyed God's commandments. So they fell away from God's way, resulting in our downfall and troubles (Genesis 3).

We have been repeating their mistake of disobeying God ever since. Hence have been paying the same price: human sorrow, decay and death. Indeed, all humans have sinned against God, no exceptions (except, of course, the Son of God: Jesus Christ – see 2 Corinthians 5:21, John 1:29 and Romans 3:22-24).

Over time, humans have shown a marked inability, like our first parents, to resist temptation from the devil. We indeed have been unable, on our own, to overcome sin along with its deadly consequences. We need God. Because of His love for us, God could not abandon us to the terrible consequences of sin. He had a solution. "For God so loved the world, that he gave his only begotten Son, that whosoever believeth in him should not perish, but have everlasting life" (John 3:16, KJV). Praise the Lord God!

The Last Adam Shows Us How to Resist Sin

Described as the last Adam, the Son of God Jesus came to give us eternal life by paying the price for our sins. "And so it is written, 'The first man Adam became a living being.' The last Adam became a life-giving spirit" (1 Corinthians 15:45, NKJV). Fruitful for eternal life, Jesus Christ sets a great example for us to follow in obeying God's law, God's way. Resisting sin successfully, the Lord Jesus demonstrated a lifestyle of love, giving and humility.

As recorded in the Holy Bible, Jesus showed us how to resist the devil's enticements to turn us away from God. In an encounter with the devil recorded in Matthew 4, Jesus resisted temptation by accurately citing and obeying the commandments of God. He resisted the devil's distortion of God's commandments with His *precise knowledge of God's true way*, God's law.

Certainly, the best way to spot a counterfeit is to be so familiar with the original that the fakes stand out. So it is with God's word, God's law. When we know it well, by God's grace, we can more readily spot and defeat devilish schemes, deceptions and distortions.

Indeed, to be familiar with God's way and avoid being deceived, it helps to *always study the Holy Bible while praying to God for the Holy Spirit to reveal its mysteries*. (Note the presence and work of the Holy Spirit when Jesus Christ walked the earth in human form – see Matthew 3:16, Mark 1:10, John 1:33 and Romans 8:11.) We need the Holy Spirit to help us stand firm and succeed in God's way.

Like Jesus, we too can resist the devil by standing firm in God's way, enabled by God's power. As the apostle Paul indicated, God's full armor includes truth, righteousness, the gospel of peace, the shield of faith, the helmet of salvation and the sword of the Spirit (the word of God – see Ephesians 6:14-18). Under the direction of the Holy Spirit, prayerfully, we *win by standing steadfast in our faith*.

Overall, we certainly must stand vigilant against devilish schemes and temptations. "Be sober, be vigilant; because your adversary the devil walks about like a roaring lion, seeking whom he may devour. Resist him, steadfast in the faith, knowing that the same sufferings are experienced by your brotherhood in the world" (1 Peter 5:8-9, NKJV). When we stand strong in our faith in God, aided by the Holy Spirit, we are impregnable, able to overcome all obstacles and enemies – praise God!

God's Protection Available to All

God's protection is available to all that seek His help. To get God's help today (if you are not saved) is quite easy. Simply "confess with your mouth the Lord Jesus and believe in your heart that God has raised Him from the dead, you will be saved. For *with the heart one believes unto righteousness*, and with the mouth confession is made unto salvation" (Romans 10:9-10, NKJV, emphasis added; see also Luke 6:45 and Matthew 12:34). Through Jesus Christ, we are able to stand redeemed instead of being condemned forever when we get saved – praise God!

Believing "unto righteousness" entails embracing God's way as revealed in the examples and teachings of Jesus Christ recorded in the Holy Bible. Indeed, believers are saved by God's grace from sin and death through the sacrifice at the cross by Jesus Christ. Because we cannot obtain righteousness (obey God's commandments completely and perfectly) in our own strength, God offers the atonement for sin by Jesus Christ. In addition, God provides the Holy Spirit working in our hearts to transform us for good.

In this loving sacrifice by Jesus Christ, we find a righteousness that comes by faith (see Romans 3:21-22, Philippians 3:9 and Romans 1:17). Through faith in God, by believing in the Lord Jesus Christ, we are saved (see Acts 11:17 and Acts 16:31). We get eternal life, defeating sin and death forever – praise God! Indeed, "for with the heart a person believes, resulting in righteousness, and with the mouth he confesses, resulting in salvation" (Romans 10:10, NASB – see also the chapter "Salvation: Life in Abundance for Ever").

Change and Victory: Our Hearts and the Holy Spirit

Significantly, God's solution for sin and death goes deep, affecting the heart. The condition of our desperately wicked hearts must be addressed (see Jeremiah 17:9). Or there would be no difference, no fundamental change within us. To help us, God puts the Holy Spirit "in our hearts" (2 Corinthians 1:22, NASB). Truly, believers can rest assured that "the love of God has been poured out within our hearts through the Holy Spirit who was given to us" (Romans 5:5, NASB; see also Matthew 22:37-40 and Romans 13:10).

As part of the salvation plan, the Lord God empowers us, enhances us through the Holy Spirit. We get to *know better* and to *do better in love*. A lifestyle of sinning (i.e., malice, greed and arrogance) thus becomes unacceptable. It indeed becomes disquieting to us as the Spirit helps to change our passions and proclivities.

Under the Holy Spirit, believers undergo a process of being molded, transformed to become ultimately like the Son of God in love, perfection and holiness. The transformation and our victory occurs not in our own strength.

"'Not by might nor by power, but by My Spirit,' says the LORD of hosts" (Zechariah 4:6, NASB).

With God's Spirit working out our transformation, we become born again, able to start a new and better life on a clean slate. God uses the Holy Spirit to maintain our walk in the way of righteousness (see the chapter: "The Holy Spirit: Power, Love and Self-Control"). The Spirit enables us to stay away from our old ways that lead to sin, sorrows and death.

Certainly, our protection for eternal life lies in coming under "the law of the Spirit of life in Christ Jesus" (see Romans 8:2, NKJV, and the chapter: "Freedom: Walking in the Way, the Truth and the Life"). To benefit from the law of the Spirit of life, assuredly, we must be saved!

The Helmet of Salvation

As believers in God, we put on the "helmet of salvation" (Ephesians 6:17, NKJV). A component of the whole armor of God, salvation is strong defense against the seen and unseen dangers that this world holds for all humans. If you haven't already done so, you need to come under God's protection quickly. Don't delay.

Through His Son, God has made salvation freely available to all – praise God! You too can get the righteousness obtainable through faith in God (see Romans 1:17 and Philippians 3:9). Jesus Christ has paid the price for sin, so you don't have to. *His resurrection by the power of the Holy Spirit demonstrates God's sovereignty over sin and death.* So, you don't have to forfeit your soul for eternity. Just come to Jesus Christ now for eternal life in abundance.

The Door to Eternal Life

And as the Son of God noted in John 10:9-11 (KJV): "I am the door: by me if any man enter in, he shall be saved, and shall go in and out, and find pasture. The thief cometh not, but for to steal, and to kill, and to destroy: I am come that they might have life, and that they might have it more abundantly. I am the good shepherd: the good shepherd giveth his life for the sheep."

Jesus Christ is the door that opens for all sincerely seeking God. Please come to the door of salvation now and receive everlasting life with all its abundant benefits. Don't settle for less in a shortened life when God can give you so much more for eternity. "Eye has not seen, nor ear heard, Nor have entered into the heart of man The things which God has prepared for those who love Him" (1 Corinthians 2:9, NKJV).

For what God has prepared for those who love Him, the Bible offers some glimpses. There will be a new world, with this one passing away. There will be new heavens and a new earth. And the saved (believers) will come to live in the presence of a most loving and almighty God, with a new spiritual and incorruptible body. There will be no more sorrow, tears or death (see the chapter: "New World: No More Sorrow").

The Best Decision

Why miss out on these great benefits from God? If you are not saved, why not become a child of God today and partake of the divine nature? There is no need for you or anyone else to waste away or be a sitting duck for the devil or demons. *God can protect you.* **God loves you.** *The Lord wants to save you from all your troubles.* God can grant you access to the kingdom of heaven. In God's kingdom, you get to live in abundance, to live in the fullness of joy and pleasures forever. Make the best decision of your life today. Come to God now!

Please say this prayer now: *Dear God, I repent and forsake my sins. I acknowledge that my Lord Jesus Christ died for my sins and was resurrected by the power of the Holy Spirit. Please fill me up with the Holy Spirit so that I can live to do Your will. I desire to be in Your presence to experience that fullness of joy and pleasures forever spoken of in Psalm 16:11. Please protect and guide my steps daily, in Jesus name I pray: Amen!*

Discussion Questions

1. How can you come under and stay under God's protection for eternal life? How can the Holy Spirit help you in this regard?

2. Who are the holy angels and how has God used them on behalf of humans under His protection? Who are the fallen angels and what are their intentions towards us?

3. Why did God put the Holy Spirit "in our hearts" (2 Corinthians 1:22, NASB)? How does God's love "poured out within our hearts through the Holy Spirit" (Romans 5:5, NASB) help overcome our desperately wicked hearts (Jeremiah 17:9)?

Chapter 24

Satisfaction

Satisfaction beyond Measure

Highlights:

- God has placed a deep-rooted hunger for eternity in all human hearts. Only the Creator can satisfy that hunger: it is a God-sized vacuum.
- We all have a choice: to follow or reject God's direction for satisfying that hunger. Based on selfless love, the Lord's way leads to everlasting fulfillment. It enables us to enjoy life to the fullest in love, righteousness, peace and joy forever.
- Those who reject God's way can never find enduring satisfaction. Their preoccupation with temporary substitutes only provokes a desperate, depressing and debilitating quest for more of the same in futilities.

One day as they were walking past "a beautiful, huge office building," Jack Graham asked his friend: "What company is that?" The answer was instructive. "Well, there's nobody in that building. It's vacant... and it's been vacant since the day it was built".

Graham wondered why such an "immaculate" structure stayed deserted. The friend explained: "That building is a monument to greed. You see, it was built before the economy collapsed with big hopes of being filled with businesses. But they haven't been able to lease one space out" (Graham, 2012).

Greed can leave people stuck with an empty building and an empty life. It never truly satisfies. That is because greed (like hatred and arrogance) counteracts God's way of loving, giving and humility. It therefore cannot endure. But God's way rooted in love endures forever. God's way is the right way to eternal life. It is the way of righteousness, granting access to the kingdom of heaven forever.

For sure, only God's kingdom will endure for eternity. It will supersede all governments, entities and societies: all spiritual, political or economic powers. There will be "new heavens and a new earth in which *righteousness dwells*" (2 Peter 3:13, ESV, emphasis added). Indeed, the world we see today will pass away. But the kingdom of heaven stays forever. Since the greedy or covetous cannot enter God's kingdom (see Ephesians 5:5), they can never obtain enduring, eternal satisfaction.

Fundamentally, we all have a deep-rooted yearning for the eternal because God "has **put eternity** in" all our hearts (Ecclesiastes 3:11, NKJV, bold emphasis added). The billion dollar question then is: what can fill that yearning: that void, that gap? Can riches fill our hunger for eternity? Maybe Power? Perhaps status? Career? Sex? Or serial relationships? Or something else? We humans, sadly, have tried throughout the ages to find satisfaction in all these, but have failed woefully. Indeed, a popular old song encapsulates that failure with the line: I can't get no satisfaction.

If the human hunger for eternity is not satisfied, then failure, frustration and dissatisfaction are sure outcomes for us. Only God's eternal kingdom and His righteousness can fill our hunger, our deep-rooted need for eternity. For as Jesus Christ Himself noted: "Blessed are *those who hunger and thirst for righteousness,* for *they shall be satisfied*" (Matthew 5:6, NASB, bold emphasis added).

To be satisfied ultimately, we must seek first God's kingdom and His righteousness (see Matthew 6:33). And in the kingdom of God, we find all that we need for eternity. In fact, we will find "righteousness and peace and joy in the Holy Spirit" (see Romans 14:17, ESV).

Basically, it is in salvation into God's kingdom that we can satisfy our deep hunger for eternity (eternal life). Salvation indeed brings eternal life. And it is obtained in "the righteousness of God through faith in Jesus Christ for all who believe" (Romans 3:22, ESV; see also Philippians 3:9 and Romans 10:9-13). *Salvation is therefore the key to obtaining satisfaction forever.* Praise God!

Love and the Kingdom of Heaven

Significantly, *selfless love is at the core of God's kingdom and His righteousness.* Love entails an attitude of giving. It entails generosity not greediness or covetousness. *Love requires that we help people, not hurt them.* We are, thankfully, aided by the Holy Spirit to walk in God's way, God's law grounded in love.

God's way entails that we connect with and listen to Jesus Christ who demonstrated God's love in action perfectly. "This is my beloved Son, with whom I am well pleased; listen to him," God told the early disciples of Jesus Christ (Matthew 17:5, ESV). By following the teachings (and example) of Jesus Christ, we can overcome the pull of sin as evident in hatred, greed and arrogance. Helped by the Holy Spirit, we get to defeat sin ultimately forever – praise God!

With the help of Jesus Christ working through the Holy Spirit, we can indeed defeat sin (and death). We can walk in the right way, in obedience to God's law: *embracing love as a lifestyle, in humility and generosity.* We thus are enabled by God to reject the wrong way: sin, typified by malice, selfishness and pride.

See Galatians 5 for details on the wrong way as opposed to the right way in terms of human conduct. The right way, the way of righteousness, produces the fruit of the Spirit (Galatians 5:22-24). The wrong way, conversely, is evident in the works or deeds of the flesh: "those who do such things will not inherit the kingdom of God" (Galatians 5:21, ESV; see also Galatians 5:19-20).

Righteousness by Faith through Love

Through Jesus Christ, we can walk in the right way (in love): we obtain a righteousness that comes by faith. This is faith in the power of God's love to make us better (see John 3:16). By God's grace through Jesus Christ, believers get eternal life and are enabled to manifest the fruit of the Spirit, with love at the core. As the apostle Paul wrote: "For in Christ Jesus neither circumcision nor uncircumcision counts for anything, but *only faith working through love*" (Galatians 5:6, ESV, bold emphasis added).

Additionally: "By this we know love, that he laid down his life for us, and we ought to lay down our lives for the brothers" (1 John 3:16, ESV). With the Holy Spirit working in us, we are able to do so. Producing the fruit of the

Spirit, we can come ultimately to love like the Son of God, truly reflecting God's image accurately.

Significantly, because we cannot fulfill God's commandments perfectly on our own, we need help. We cannot love perfectly, so we need someone who can: Jesus Christ, the Son of God. A perfect example, He helps us to love as God loves. We can therefore confidently put our faith in Him (see Romans 3:22). Overall, Jesus Christ empowers us through the Holy Spirit (as work-in progress) for the ultimate goal: *to love perfectly like God.*

Indeed, through Jesus Christ, to reiterate a key point, we find the **righteousness** that comes by faith "*working through love*" (see Philippians 3:9, Galatians 5:5-14, Mark 12:28-34 and Romans 3:21-22). And remember that *satisfaction comes to those who* "hunger and thirst for **righteousness**" (see Matthew 5:6, NASB). God works it all out perfectly – praise the Lord!

Aiming High in Life

Now, *let's be clear* about this chapter's opening story. Erecting big and beautiful buildings is not bad in of itself. If the motive is right based on God's standards, we can and should strive for bigger and better things.

We definitely can aim for greater heights of achievements. In fact, we should be aiming heavenwards "looking unto Jesus, the author and finisher of *our* faith, who for the joy that was set before Him endured the cross, despising the shame, and has sat down at the right hand of the throne of God" (Hebrews 12:2, NKJV).

Attaining Our Full Potential in God

Through Jesus Christ, we can aspire to and actually attain our full potential. *Created in God's image* (see Genesis 1:26), our full potential is in God. Because *God is love* (see 1 John 4:8), we ought to reflect God, replicating His love. Anything less than reflecting God in love will disappoint and produce dissatisfaction. Unfortunately, all humans fall short (see Romans 3:23).

Solution: to realize our full potential, and be satisfied ultimately, we ought to be more like our most righteous God in holiness and perfection. "Be ye therefore perfect, even as your Father which is in heaven is perfect" (Matthew

5:48, KJV). Moreover: "You shall be holy, for I the Lord your God am holy" (Leviticus 19:2, NASB).

That's *the essence of our full potential: walking in* **love,** **holiness** *and* **perfection,** *producing* **good works** (see Ephesians 2:10). Anything less brings dissatisfaction. Unfortunately, sin has so damaged us, we don't accurately reflect God's image. That is why so many people cannot find satisfaction. They are operating less than their full potential. (Sorry, but an eagle can never be satisfied functioning as a chicken!)

To help us, out of His infinite love, mercy and grace, God works out our salvation through Jesus Christ to enable us fulfill our full potential. Believers are enabled, molded to become more like God. It's a process that helps us eventually to become perfect and holy, *flowing in good works underscored by love.* Through the Holy Spirit – the Spirit of power, love and self-control (see 2 Timothy 1:7) – we can operate beyond our own capabilities. We can come to *love our neighbors as ourselves* and *do no harm to them* (see Romans 13:9-10, Matthew 22:34-40, Galatians 5:14-15 and Leviticus 19:17-18). Praise God!

Satisfaction through Good Works

Through the Holy Spirit, God helps us to forsake our old bad habits. Typically driven by malice, greed and arrogance, these habits breed dissatisfaction because they do not reflect God's image. By God's grace, we can certainly overcome our old habits. Empowered by the Lord, we get to focus on *doing good works, underscored by love, generosity and humility* – praise God! It is through good works – propelled by love, holiness and perfection – that we get to fulfill our full potential, and hence obtain enduring satisfaction.

Fundamentally, *we are designed for good works* – not evil works! "For we are His workmanship, *created in Christ Jesus for good works, which God prepared beforehand so that we would walk in them*" (Ephesians 2:10, NASB, emphasis added). God created us to walk in good works. That's what we are built for. We can never be satisfied walking otherwise.

In fact, a sure way to guarantee a life of dissatisfaction is to waste time in sin, engaging in evil works. In sin, you do harm to others. In sin, you do **not** love your neighbors as yourself. In sin, you are a loser, forever. A lifestyle of sinning, of evil works, will leave you miserable in the end. Satisfaction will elude you forever. That's because *you are **not** designed for evil works*. You are made for good works.

You are created in God's image. And *God is love!* Walking in a mode apart from love means you are working against yourself. In that mode, you are in conflict with *the image of love that you are modeled after*. You can never be satisfied in that mode. Neither will you have peace. A change hence is required for you to obtain enduring satisfaction through salvation. You need to be born again, transformed for everlasting life (see the chapter "Born Again: Rebirth into Eternity, a Fresh Start").

When you become saved (a believer in God), thankfully, you undergo a huge transformation. You are molded by the Holy Spirit to reflect more the essence of God's image. *It's the image of love, of righteousness.* It is the image of the Ultimate Giver of good gifts who has power, self-control, humility, perfection and holiness, flowing in good works. By reflecting that image aided by the Holy Spirit, we can find enduring satisfaction – praise God!

The Ultimate Satisfaction: Becoming Like God

To be *satisfied ultimately*, you must become holy like God, perfect in love, having eternal life and full of good works. Anything less will not satisfy. "An ultimate commitment to anything less than ultimate will not ultimately satisfy," says author Norman L. Geisler in a presentation titled *The Importance of Knowing the True God.*

Indeed, to fulfil your full potential by reflecting God's image, your future must be secured in the kingdom of heaven. Therein lies your ultimate satisfaction. God is eternal. So is His kingdom. By becoming saved, you too can have eternal life, with access to God's kingdom forever and all its abundant benefits (see the chapter titled: "Salvation: Life in Abundance Forever").

Significantly, anything less than becoming like God in love, holiness, perfection and immortality will lead to disappointment. Indeed, the more like God you become, the more you can become satisfied ultimately. But you must first know God.

"We can't be like God unless we know what God is like," notes Geisler (be sure to contact him for the excellent presentation: www.normgeisler.com). And we know from the Bible that God is love. To know God truly, we must love. *"Anyone who does not love does not know God, because God is love"* (1 John

4:8, ESV, emphasis added). Thankfully, God helps us to get to know Him. We just need to be *sincere in seeking Him* and He will take care of the rest (see the chapter: "The Knowledge of God" and Psalm 145:18).

God's help is essential because our own strength, our own wisdom is inadequate. So the Lord helps us with the Holy Spirit to empower and enlighten us. Through the Spirit, we become born again. It is only by being born again that we can enter the kingdom of heaven (see the chapter "Born Again: Rebirth into Eternity, a Fresh Start").

The Holy Spirit comes to dwell within believers, taking us step-by-step through the things we need to change to become more like God in love. The Spirit helps us on the journey to becoming more loving and less hurtful to others.

Perfection: Loving Like God

Loving like God does require meeting a standard of love, of perfection, that's difficult given our weaknesses. It certainly takes more than human strength to love like God. That is so true, especially since it may involve loving your enemies, not just your friends! And that's why we need the Holy Spirit, the Spirit of power, love and self-control (see 2 Timothy 1:7).

"But I say to you, **love your enemies** and pray for those who persecute you, so that you may be sons of your Father who is in heaven; for **He causes His sun to rise on** *the* **evil and** *the* **good, and sends rain on** *the* **righteous and** *the* **unrighteous.** For if you love those who love you, what reward do you have? Do not even the tax collectors do the same? If you greet only your brothers, what more are you doing *than others*? Do not even the Gentiles do the same? Therefore you are to be **perfect**, as your heavenly Father is perfect" so said Jesus (Matthew 5:44-48, NASB, bold emphasis added).

God's way of perfection anchored in love, if embraced by all, can produce a perfect world. But not everyone sees things God's way. That is why so many people are doomed to unhappiness and dissatisfaction. Through God's way, assuredly, you'll find everlasting satisfaction.

Embracing God's Way

By following God's way, we are saved from the second death. Believers gain eternal life, inheriting the kingdom of heaven and its many great benefits.

Anyone with a mindset or lifestyle that ignores this simple fact about life and death is asking for disappointment and disaster.

But for believers, the focus through the gospel of salvation is on God's everlasting kingdom. Believers, therefore, possess a God-given sense of calmness through life's storms (see the chapter "Peace beyond Understanding"). Consequently, the ups and downs of this present life do not faze believers. We are empowered to remain content regardless of the conditions. Believers operate under a divine assurance that all things will turn out good for us eventually (see Romans 8:28) – praise God!

The Danger of Rejecting God's Way

But all things *won't* turn out good for those who do not love God or walk in His way of love. For they show evil works, doing harm to others, hence cannot claim to be "called according to *His* purpose" (Romans 8:28, NASB). Condemned to the second death, unbelievers miss eternal life. Death shortchanges their dreams, aspirations and satisfaction. *There is no genuine satisfaction when you end up dead, with no hope for salvation.*

The bottom line is this: the soul that sins must die (see Genesis 3:3, Ezekiel 18:20 and Romans 8:13). All humans are guilty. We have all fallen short of God's glory (see Romans 3:23 and Romans 5:12-19). In our fallen state, we don't make the cut to fit His image of love, perfection and holiness. So we all are condemned to die forever, except those saved by God's grace through Jesus Christ – praise God!

At one point while on earth, the Son of God posed this very crucial question: "For what profit is it to a man if he gains the whole world, and loses his own soul? Or what will a man give in exchange for his soul" (Matthew 16:26, NKJV)? In essence, if all your strivings in life leads to great achievements (from a human perspective) but leaves out the fate of the soul, you basically have gained nothing.

You need more than worldly achievements *to satisfy the deep yearning for eternity that God has planted in the human heart.* There is certainly more to us than our body. In all, *we are spirit, soul and body* (see 1 Thessalonians 5:23). Any pursuit in life that ignores this basic fact will fail! Why focus on taking care of the body solely? *Why neglect the soul? Why neglect the spiritual realm?* Why ignore eternity?

At the End of the Road: Life beyond Death

At the end of the road, those who ignore God's way of love suffer miserably. They do not seek first God's eternal kingdom and His righteousness. Because their priorities are mixed up, they end up *not* living up to their full potential in God. Their end is eternal failure, sadly, unable to achieve God's purpose in their lives.

Yes, God has a specific plan, a purpose for everyone (see the chapter "Purpose: Directions for Life"). It is dangerous not to seek diligently what that purpose is. Emptiness and dissatisfaction are guaranteed if you don't seek God's guidance.

When God is not in the picture, your aspirations will be misdirected. They will eventually evaporate, simply fading into nothingness, an abyss that permanently sucks away desire, hope, fulfillment and life. *Sadly, those who ignore God, His kingdom and His righteousness, can never be satisfied.*

They say death and taxes are guaranteed to all. But there is life after death provided by God (see John 3:16, Revelations 20-21, Matthew 10:28, Luke 12:4-5 and Hebrews 9:27-28). The dead in Christ are assured of resurrection into eternal life: "over these the second death has no power" (Revelation 20:6, NASB). But nonbelievers will perish forever (see 2 Thessalonians 1:9).

The Benefits of Lining up Our Priorities Right

For those saved (believers), eternal life holds a beautiful harvest of *everlasting* love, joy, peace, fulfillment and pleasures. With a renewed mindset, believers come to understand how temporary this world is. This understanding frees us to focus time, talents and treasures on what really counts for eternity. It's a focus that minimizes and eliminates unnecessary distractions and worries.

Those distracted by worries about fulfilling their needs in this world should consider the reference Jesus made to how God feeds the birds (Matthew 6:25-26). Humans are more valuable to God than the birds. *God places such a great value on us that He sent His Son Jesus Christ to die for our sins – praise God!*

The plan of salvation demonstrates how much worth God places on our souls, for He takes no pleasure in our destruction. "'For I have no pleasure in the death of anyone who dies,' says the Lord God. 'Therefore, repent and live'" (Ezekiel 18:32, NASB).

Consider this: *if God can give so much to save us through Jesus Christ,* why would He then abandon us in the daily needs of this world? So don't worry, if you are a believer in God. Your needs will be met. Your satisfaction is guaranteed.

When to Worry and How to Deal with It

But *if you are **not** saved, you do have every reason to worry.* You will miss out on the everlasting benefits available only to those who seek first the kingdom of God and His righteousness, above all else. So please change, if you haven't already done so. Get saved: become born again. Become a believer in God. Cry out to Jesus now to save you. Start now to put God first in your life! If you do, you will have no need to worry about your needs being fulfilled.

When you become saved, you can trust in the provisions God has made for His children (believers). "For your heavenly Father knows that you need all these things. *But seek first the kingdom of God and His righteousness, and all these things shall be added to you*" (Matthew 6:33, NKJV, emphasis added). The promise for "all these things" are for God's children, those who put God first in their lives. Know that if you are not saved, you are **not** a child of God (see John 1:12). But you can get saved now easily. Just cry out to God in Jesus name!

Fundamentally, when you put God first in your life, you get everything – all the eternal benefits of God. Assuredly, when the kingdom of God becomes your focus – your priority number one – all things eventually fall into place in a wonderful way (see the chapter "Priority Number One: God – His Kingdom and His Righteousness"). Significantly, you come to grasp a realistic perspective on life underscored by the understanding that only God's kingdom will survive eventually. Beware: this world is passing away!

A Fading World: What Are You Attached To?

God will be creating a new earth and new heavens (see Isaiah 66:22, Isaiah 65:17 and 2 Peter 3:10-13). By understanding that this world is fading away, believers can through the Holy Spirit resist getting attached to this world and its temporary things. Those things won't last anyway, so why get attached?

When we get hooked on temporary things in search of enduring satisfaction, guess what happens? Disappointment is certain. Don't expect permanent satisfaction. Our focus should be on God. We are to *love God* (who is everlasting and requires us to *love people*). We are indeed to focus on God's kingdom, and His righteousness, which is everlasting. We should *not* make this world our priority number one. We should definitely not love this temporary world.

In this light, we should all heed the words of the apostle John: "Do not love the world nor the things in the world. If anyone loves the world, the love of the Father is not in him. For all that is in the world, the *lust of the flesh* and the *lust of the eyes* and the *boastful pride of life,* is not from the Father, but is from the world. *The world is passing away*, and *also* its lusts; but the one *who does the will of God lives forever*" (1 John 2:15-17, NASB, bold emphasis added). Only investments in the things of *our eternal God* are guaranteed to yield eternal returns and bring everlasting satisfaction (see Matthew 6:19-33).

What's on Your Mind?

For everlasting satisfaction, crucially, we must be mindful of what we sow in our minds. Our thoughts can breed distractions and disaffections, diverting us from what truly counts for eternity. "Finally, brethren, whatever things are **true**, whatever things *are* **noble**, whatever things *are* **just**, whatever things *are* **pure**, whatever things *are* **lovely**, whatever things *are* of **good report**, if *there is* any **virtue** and if *there is* anything **praiseworthy—meditate on these things**" (Philippians 4:8, NKJV, bold emphasis added).

For meditating on the above, consequently, "the God of peace shall be with you" (Philippians 4:9, KJV). In the space of divine peace, we can stand joyful and secure forever. We cannot be rocked or moved by the internal or external turmoil that robs many of their sense of peace, achievement, fulfillment or satisfaction.

With help from the Holy Spirit, thankfully, believers cannot be overrun by the disquiet that disrupts and ruins those who are focused on ungodly things. Believers are instead *focused* on the good, the loving, the holy, the perfect, the joyful, the true, the noble, the fulfilling, the heavenly – the everlasting. For as a person thinks, so is he/she (Proverbs 23:7). *An earth-bound mindset is doomed just like this earth* (see 2 Peter 3:10).

A Focus on God's Law (Love): a Heavenly Mindset

Indeed, our focus, our meditation needs to be on God's message in the Bible, pointing us to the kingdom of heaven. With this focus, we are planting seeds in our minds that will yield enduring benefits in God. Meditating on God's message promotes a heavenly mindset that counteracts sin and its consequences.

As the Psalmist wrote: "Your word I have treasured in my heart, That I may not sin against You" (Psalm 119:11, NASB). Sin diminishes, destroys our love, joy, peace, prosperity, success and satisfaction. It can cost us our lives ultimately. We must avoid it by embracing God's law grounded in love.

Indicating how important God's law is, God told Joshua when he succeeded Moses: "This book of the law shall not depart from your mouth, but you shall *meditate on it day and night, so that you may be careful to do according to all that is written in it*; for then you will make your way prosperous, and then you will have success" (Joshua 1:8, NASB – emphasis added).

Godly prosperity and success breeds enduring satisfaction. Surely, "The blessing of the Lord makes rich, and he adds no sorrow with it" (Proverbs 10:22, ESV). In addition, as Psalm 1:1-3 (NASB) records:

> "How blessed is the man who does not walk in the counsel
> of the wicked,
> Nor stand in the path of sinners,
> Nor sit in the seat of scoffers!
> But his delight is in the law of the LORD,
> And in His law he meditates day and night.
> He will be like a tree *firmly* planted by streams of water,
> Which yields its fruit in its season
> And its leaf does not wither;
> And in whatever he does, he prospers."

If your mind is set heavenwards through meditating on and applying the law of God, you will definitely find enduring prosperity, success and satisfaction.

The Big Picture

God knows what we need. The Lord understands what we all yearn for at the very core of our beings. After all, God designed us. And He wants us to be fulfilled, to gain enduring success and satisfaction. So He helps us. That's because He loves us.

Through Jesus Christ, God enables us to attain our full potential. The Son of God points the way clearly, emphasizing the importance of setting our priorities right in God. *We are to hunger and thirst for righteousness, seeking first God's kingdom and His righteousness, based on love* (see Matthew 5:6, Matthew 6:33, Matthew 22:36-40, Ephesians 5:1-21 and Galatians 5). God shall definitely supply all of our needs when we put our trust and priority in Him (see Philippians 4:19, Matthew 6:33 and Proverbs 3:5-10).

By setting our priorities right in God, we embrace the eternity perspective. We see the big picture. *There is more to life than this world which is passing away. You too* can see the big picture (if you don't already). Know that if you are not yet saved, you are cut off from eternal life. You will miss the kingdom of heaven. You therefore can never be satisfied. You can however change that right now by asking Jesus Christ to come into your life. Why wait? This world is passing away. *You don't want to be among those who pass away with it.* Please don't ignore the fate of your soul.

Filling a God-Sized Vacuum

When we ignore the fate of our soul for eternity, we tend to end up in harm's way. We end up distracted with pursuits that can become bloated, life-sucking endeavors that mask a dangerous emptiness inside. It is a God-sized vacuum that only the Creator of the universe can fill. A world of power, property, prosperity or prominence gained outside of God's pathway will not last and cannot fill that emptiness. The eternity perspective – our need for eternal life – is too important to brush aside.

To attain true satisfaction, genuine contentment, everlasting joy, the way to go is to devote your time, talents and treasures to God: His kingdom and His righteousness. He gives you everything you need to make that devotion anyway. So there is really no point in losing your soul.

You can gain so much more from the everlasting benefits in God. If you are not saved, make the move today and start living for God right now. By God's grace, you can secure a place in the kingdom of heaven. Why not become a child of God, a partaker of the divine nature and a joint heir with the Son of God?

Please say this prayer now: *Dear God, please help me and set me free from the law of sin and death. Help me to get on the right path to everlasting life, enduring satisfaction. I acknowledge and repent of my sins – please forgive me. I accept Jesus Christ as my Lord and Savior, and acknowledge that He died for my sins and was resurrected by the Holy Spirit. Please fill me up with the Holy Spirit so that I can live to do Your will. In Jesus name I pray, Amen!*

Reference

• Graham, J. (2012). How to choose contentment over greed. *LightSource*. Retrieved from http://www.lightsource.com/devotionals/powerpoint-with-jack-graham/powerpoint-june-29-2012-11673016.html).

Discussion Questions

1. What exactly is the eternity perspective and how is it connected to the right mindset for enduring satisfaction? What does it mean to say: God "has put eternity in" all our hearts (Ecclesiastes 3:11, NKJV)? And why did Jesus say: "Blessed are those who hunger and thirst for righteousness, for they shall be satisfied" (Matthew 5:6, NASB)? How is that connected to seeking first the kingdom of God and His righteousness (Matthew 6:33)?

2. What is true, enduring satisfaction and why has it been so elusive for many humans? How can you get everlasting satisfaction? How is that connected to achieving your full potential as one created in God's image?

3. How does love, perfection, holiness and good works in God fit into the big picture of eternity – how does seeing the big picture help with obtaining enduring satisfaction? How is the Spirit of power, love and self-control involved? And how does the Holy Spirit help you resist the way of hatred, greed and arrogance?

Chapter 25

New World

New World: No More Sorrow

Highlights:

- Jesus Christ is coming back to usher in a new world, making all things new, with the kingdom of God replacing forever all political, economic, social or spiritual powers.
- Believers will get to dwell with God, without sin and death, with no more pain, tears or sorrow – there will be new heavens and a new earth: praise God!
- When the Son of God comes back, the saved (believers in God) will inherit a new spiritual and incorruptible body, living in the love, splendor, joy and beauty of God's presence forever. Hallelujah!

"But the day of the Lord will come as a thief in the night, in which the heavens will pass away with a great noise, and the elements will melt with fervent heat; both the earth and the works that are in it will be burned up," so wrote the apostle Peter, an early follower of Jesus Christ, foretelling the fate of our world (2 Peter 3:10, NKJV; see also Isaiah 65:17, Revelation 21:1 and Isaiah 66:22).

"Therefore, since all these things will be dissolved, what manner of persons ought you to be in holy conduct and godliness, looking for and hastening the coming of the day of God, because of which the heavens will be dissolved, being on fire, and the elements will melt with fervent heat? Nevertheless we, according to His promise, *look for new heavens and a new earth in which righteousness dwells*," Peter added (2 Peter 3:11-13, NKJV, emphasis added).

That is the sad reality of the world we live in today. It will all come to an end! The world as we know it will pass away. The earth and all its magnificent structures will not survive. All the great treasures on earth will perish. Yet out of this dismal fate, there is hope. God will provide replacement: a new earth. Just imagine the size of what God plans to do. The vastness of this earth will be replaced with a new one! Even the heavens will not stay untouched, unshaken. Essentially, we'll be getting a new world. (Note that my term "new world" may be inadequate to describe what God is going to do.)

For those who are saved, the Lord indeed has great plans. Believers get to be free of all the sorrows, diseases, shame, negatives and evil that have so polluted, corrupted, distorted and diminished this world. Its destruction is inevitable. Yes, there will be "new heavens and a new earth in which righteousness dwells" (2 Peter 3:13, ESV). In the new world, death is no more – praise God! We get true freedom, no longer bond to a mortal body of sin and death! Love prevails! Glory to God!

Living with God Forever

The most fascinating and wonderful experience of the expected new world promises to be *God coming to dwell among believers*. There is indescribable love, joy, peace, beauty, wonder, purity, perfection and holiness in the presence of God. We are talking about the God who created our wonderful, stunning galaxies. It is the same God who created diamonds, gold and other precious objects. This is the God who created the beautiful splendor we see in the magnificent life forms and floral patterns on land, sea and air. Believers get to dwell in the presence of this same loving God! Wow! Wow again!

"And I heard a loud voice from the throne, saying, 'Behold, the tabernacle of God is among men, and He will dwell among them, and they shall be His people, and God Himself will be among them, and He will wipe away every tear from their eyes; and there will no longer be *any* death; there will no longer be *any* mourning, or crying, or pain; the first things have passed away," wrote the apostle John, foretelling future events as given to the resurrected Christ by God (Revelation 21:3-4, NASB; see also Revelation 1). What a wonderful God we serve!

Love, Beauty, Joy and Pleasures Forever

We are talking about a God of immeasurable love. God *is* love. Believers get to live with *love*, the ultimate in love. We get to be with Jesus Christ, His Son, who showed us His love by dying for our sins (while we were yet sinners). While we were far off, God would do so much for us, with the sacrifice at the cross. How much more would the Lord then do for us when we come to live so close, and so near? So dear! Praise God!

In God's presence, we get to experience His love as we have never before. Believers do now experience it with the Holy Spirit in us – expect more! What a great promise to look forward to. That God would want to bring us that close to Himself, embracing us as children, taking care of our every need. That is true love! All praises to God for His mercy, love and grace! Blessed be the name of our Lord and Savior Jesus Christ! Believers are truly blessed beyond measure. We have so much to look forward to and much more to thank God for! All praises to the only wise and good God, the Lord of heaven and earth!

And as King David wrote: "One thing have I desired of the Lord, that will I seek after; that I may dwell in the house of the Lord all the days of my life, to behold the beauty of the Lord, and to enquire in his temple" (Psalm 27:4, KJV). Moreover: "You make known to me the path of life; in your presence there is fullness of joy; at your right hand are pleasures forevermore" (Psalm 16:11, ESV). In God's presence, there is joy in fullness, pleasures forever and perfect beauty.

New Spiritual Body

In the new world, believers thankfully get a new spiritual body. This present one inherited from Adam has been beaten and battered by sin. The new body will be incorruptible, no longer doomed to the limitations of the present one that is plagued by sin, disease and death. Believers get to bear the image of the heavenly Man – the last Adam: Jesus Christ. We get to be like the Son of God, ultimately inheriting His qualities. Believers are joint heirs of God with Jesus Christ. What great, undeserved blessings! We cannot but praise God! Hallelujah!

"So also is the resurrection of the dead. It is sown a perishable body, it is raised an *imperishable* body; it is sown in dishonor, it is raised in *glory*; it is sown in weakness, it is raised in *power*; it is sown a natural body, it is raised a

spiritual body. If there is a natural body, there is also a spiritual body. So also it is written, 'The first man, Adam, became a living soul.' The last Adam became a life-giving spirit," so wrote the apostle Paul (1 Corinthians 15:42-45, NASB, bold emphasis added).

A New Jerusalem

There will also be a new Jerusalem. In the vision of future events, the apostle John "saw the holy city" the "new Jerusalem, coming down from God out of heaven, prepared as a bride adorned for her husband" (Revelation 21:2, KJV). The new holy city, John noted, has "the glory of God: and her light was like unto a stone most precious, even like a jasper stone, clear as crystal..." (Revelation 21:11, KJV). What is striking about this coming reality is how much focus the world is placing on the current city of Jerusalem. People are prepared to kill and die over control of the current Jerusalem, yet God is going to replace it with a new one from heaven.

The new Jerusalem will be illuminated by God's presence, among other amazingly unique characteristics. "I saw no temple in it, for the Lord God the Almighty and the Lamb are its temple. And the city has no need of the sun or of the moon to shine on it, *for the glory of God has illumined it, and its lamp is the Lamb.* The nations will walk by its light, and the kings of the earth will bring their glory into it. In the daytime (for there will be no night there) its gates will never be closed; and they will bring the glory and the honor of the nations into it; and *nothing unclean, and no one who practices abomination and lying, shall ever come into it, but only those whose names are written in the Lamb's book of life*" (Revelation 21:22-27, NASB, emphasis added).

All Things Become New

Essentially, believers get to inherit a whole new world. It'll be free of all imperfections, sin, sorrow and death. The apostle John wrote further: "Then He who sat on the throne said, *'Behold, I make all things new.'* And He said to me, 'Write, for these words are true and faithful.' And He said to me, 'It is done! I am the Alpha and the Omega, the Beginning and the End. *I will give of the fountain of the water of life freely to him who thirsts.* He who overcomes shall *inherit all things*, and I will be his God and he shall be My son. But the cowardly, unbelieving, abominable, murderers, sexually immoral, sorcerers, idolaters, and all liars shall have their part in the lake which burns with fire and brimstone, which is the *second death*'" (Revelation 21:5-8, NKJV, emphasis added; see also Ecclesiastes 3:11 and Matthew 5:6).

Why Miss Out?

Are you saved? If not, why not? Why not become a believer in the *God who loves you* so much? Why not partake in the wonderful new world coming? Why leave yourself exposed to the wrath of God against sin? Why put your hopes in things that will not last? This world will be destroyed and everything in it.

The fate of this world should prompt you to pause. It should prompt you to reconsider your choices if your decisions have excluded God. It should generate a response of acceptance for the gospel of God, the good news of salvation from perdition. It should bring about a change of heart manifested in your attitude and actions.

Moreover, as the apostle Peter asked (2 Peter 3:11, NASB): "Since all these things are to be destroyed in this way, what sort of people ought you to be in holy conduct and godliness"? You should be moved to ask God for help. There is no need for you to suffer the fate of the doomed. You don't have to suffer the second death.

In the coming new world, only those saved (believers) will survive. The saved get to inherit the wonderful benefits of the new world, including: love, joy, peace and pleasures everlasting, with no pain, sorrow, death or tears. Why miss out? Salvation is within your grasp now (if you are not saved)! Reach out to God for help now! Make peace with God now!

Know that ***God loves you*** and wants you to enjoy all the benefits of being a child of God! Ask God to come into your life now by saying this prayer: *Dear God, please help me to become born again. I admit I am a sinner – please forgive me. I acknowledge that Jesus Christ died for my sins and was resurrected by the power of the Holy Spirit, making a way for all believers to live forever. Please fill me up with the Holy Spirit so that I can live to do Your will and enjoy all the benefits in God forever. In Jesus name I pray, amen!*

Discussion Questions

1. Why will God make all things new, with new heavens, a new earth and a new Jerusalem coming out of heaven? What's wrong with things as they are now?

2. How can a human being make it into the kingdom of heaven to live in the presence of God in all joy, love, peace, prosperity and pleasures forever?

3. Those who don't make it into the kingdom of God, what is their fate and how is that fate so dreadful it should be avoided?

About the Author

Fred Igbeare describes himself as a 'strong believer in God' proclaiming the good news of great joy. A reporter/writer/editor for many years across continents, the author sees the gospel of God as holding the ultimate solution to all human problems. The solution comes in the power of God's love replicated through humans to each other. God loves us. The Creator wants us to love each other. Our failure to love each other dooms the human race. Hatred breeds human failures. Only God's intervention can change our story from failure to success. God is offering us everlasting success and satisfaction with no more sorrows: freedom from slavery to the law of sin and death. We can get eternal life in the kingdom of heaven, critical because this world is passing away. God will create a new earth and new heavens! Only the kingdom of God will stand forever, replacing all political, economic or spiritual powers and realms existing currently. The author believes there are great benefits in deferring to God to solve human problems. We can have everlasting peace, prosperity, freedom, rest, success, satisfaction, joy and other great benefits when we come to God. The author's goal, ever the reporter, is to let people everywhere know of this good news of great benefits in God. He aims to empower fellow humans with vital information so they can have all the facts to make the right decision about life and death.